Prophecy 2017 – 2137

17 Psychic Predictions About the Coming Financial Collapse, The End of America, World War III, and the Flowering of Human Consciousness

Copyright © 2016 Mark Anastasi. All rights reserved. No portion of this book, except for brief review, may be reproduced, stored in a retrieval system, or transmitted in any form or by any means—electronic, mechanical, photocopying, recording, or otherwise—without the written permission of the publisher.

Published by
Elevation Publishing

Printed in the United States of America

ISBN-978-1-78555-005-8

"Predictions are hard, especially about the future."

Mark Twain

CONTENT

Introduction 1

Chapter 1   Prophecy of the Hopi Indian Elders 21

Chapter 2   Michael Griffiths' Prophetic Dreams of Russia and China Invading America 25

Chapter 3   Rebecca Sterling's 1999 Vision of Martial Law in America 37

Chapter 4   Mena Lee Grebin's 1987 Vision of War and Famine in the USA 41

Chapter 5   Barbara Marciniak's Prophecy of "a Flowering of Consciousness" 45

Chapter 6   Will Earth Have Fewer People? 59

Chapter 7   Credo Mutwa Predicts Global Financial Collapse and World War III (1993) 63

Chapter 8   The Prophecies of Sufi Master Naimatullah Shah Wali (1330 – 1431) 75

Chapter 9   Jamie Passmore's Prophetic Vision of World War III 81

Chapter 10   Edgar Cayce's Predicted World War III Would Arise in Syria and Turkey 85

Chapter 11   Raymond Aguilera's Prophetic Visions of the End of America and World War III 91

Chapter 12	Terry Bennett's Vision of Anarchy and Lawlessness in the US 101
Chapter 13	Dumitru Duduman's Vision of Nuclear War in America (1984) 103
Chapter 14	Polish Priest Czeslaw Klimuszko's Vision of a Cataclysmic Destruction of Europe 107
Chapter 15	Remote Viewer Ed Dames: The "Killshot" 109
Chapter 16	Joe Brandt's Vision of California Sinking Into The Pacific Ocean (1937) 113
Chapter 17	Greek Orthodox Elder Joseph of Vatopedino Warns of World War III 125
Chapter 18	Prophetic Visions of Baba Vanga Pandeva, The "Nostradamus of the Balkans" 135
Chapter 19	Will There Be a "One World Government"? 139
Chapter 20	Albert Pike's Vision of Three World Wars and "a Formidable Social Cataclysm" (1871) 145
Chapter 21	Stewart Swerdlow's Predictions (2002) 149
Chapter 22	Future Timeline Seen by Al Bielek – The Year 2137 On Earth 157
Epilogue	 161
Appendix	 167

A Warning from Russian President Vladimir Putin 167

Harry S. Dent's Predictions 173

The Great Global Monetary Reset 177

Psychic Hollywood: Is Hollywood Warning Us of What Is To Come? ... 180

A Message From Jesus Christ, Channelled by a Prophet 189

INTRODUCTION

Our taxi driver didn't even have time to hit the brakes. The 400-pound wild boar had appeared seemingly out of nowhere, and we hit it at full speed, just a mile away from our house. We were thrown about the vehicle like rag dolls. The car was totalled, much to the driver's chagrin. And the poor animal lay dying in the middle of the road, blood spurting from its snout.

* * * * * * * * * *

Thirty minutes earlier I'd experienced something unusual. My wife and I had flown home from our holiday, and during the taxi ride back to our house the driver kept looking at her in his rear-view mirror, while speaking in a loud and animated way. He was barely paying attention to the road. I didn't understand what he was saying, but he seemed to be an angry and nervous man.

Suddenly, a voice in my head – or rather a fully formed thought that did not originate from my own mind – instructed me to: *'Tell him to shut the f*** up and look ahead at the bloody road!'*. It would appear that my 'spirit guide' or 'guardian angel' doesn't shy away from using four-letter words to make his point.

Since I didn't speak the driver's language and my wife was engaged in conversation with him, I held my tongue. But I felt uneasy. A few minutes later, the thought **'OK then... brace yourself...'** entered my mind, as I was mentally shown a picture of someone raising their knees towards the driver's seat and placing their head between their arms, similar to the 'brace' position shown in airplane safety instructions.

Once again I ignored this advice, thinking it was just my imagination. Besides, we were about to reach our destination, and I didn't want to have a conversation with my wife along the lines of *"Honey, why are you curled up in a ball, in the 'brace' position?"*, let alone have to ask her to join in 'on a hunch'. A few minutes later, the driver crashed into that poor animal.

I walked the last mile to our house, shaken by the whole experience, and feeling sad for the boar and its piglets that I imagined were wondering where their daddy was. And then another thought crossed my mind.

"I don't know who that was, but… next time, I'll listen to my intuition!"

* * * * * * * * * *

As I look back on my life, I can see how in my moments of despair I was guided to take certain actions. In Oxford, England, where I worked as a security guard in my early twenties, suffering from depression and low self-esteem, I woke up one day with the thought *"Go to the Borders bookshop in town and buy books about 'Happiness'! You will begin your study of the topic called 'Happiness'!".*

I walked into the bookshop later that morning, and was directed to the self-help section. Not finding any books specifically about 'Happiness', I turned around and started heading towards the exit when I tripped over a small but hefty book titled *"GIANT STEPS"*. The toothy grin of author Anthony Robbins was looking up at me. I had literally tripped over *Giant Steps!* How ironic, I thought to myself. And what was that book even *doing* there, on the floor, in the first place? I'm certain it wasn't there when I walked in!

Introduction

Despite the book costing £6.99 – the equivalent of more than two hours of pay at my minimum wage job (£3.25 an hour) – I decided to buy it. *"If I only get ONE good idea from this book that helps my life in some way, it will have been worth the investment!"*

The book contained hundreds of tips and ideas for improving your life, including one idea that made a lot of sense to me: *'modelling success'*. Other people have achieved what *you* want to achieve, so why not model the steps they took? If I wanted to find happiness, I decided, I would model people who are happy. *How do they think? What do they say? What actions do they take? What are their habits? What do they do with their time?* This exercise would eventually change my life. *Save* my life, in fact.

This would not be the only time I would be 'guided' to buying a specific book. In 2004 I was in a bookshop in Stansted Airport, in London. I was looking at some books on the lower shelves, wanting to pick something up to read during the flight, when my left hand shot up and landed on one of the top shelves. When I looked up, I was holding the book *"The Celestine Prophecy"*, by James Redfield, in my hand. To this day I can't really explain how it happened. A surreal moment.

Over the years, I have experienced on a number of occasions having three or more random people recommend *the same book* to me within a few days of each other. I know to follow the signs now, and I order that book on Amazon on the spot. Obviously 'someone' intends for me to read it!

* * * * * * * * *

As the vibrational frequency of our planet is rising and we evolve towards a higher state of consciousness, more and more people are reporting having profound spiritual experiences.

More people are awakening their psychic and healing abilities, and those with existing abilities are seeing them enhanced.

Ever since I read the book *"Life After Life"* by Raymond Moody, at the precocious age of ten, I have been fascinated by life-after-death stories and people who possess a psychic gift. Over the years I have had the privilege of spending time with a handful of extremely gifted people. They do not take credit for the information they pass on, nor for their predictions about the future. They claim to simply be a 'channel', a *conduit* if you will, channelling information from their 'spirit guides'. Our spirit guides – they tell us – communicate with us through our intuition, dreams, and feelings, but most people today are not open to receiving these messages. Our minds are often too cluttered and busy.

These spirit guides occasionally reveal information about past lives, the truth about the nature of God… and crucially, as far as this book is concerned, *the future*.

In these pages I am sharing some particularly startling predictions by psychics and channellers about our planet's future. If their predictions are accurate and the events they describe *do* in fact take place in the future – *if they can actually foretell an event that has yet to occur!* – **our entire concept of time and space needs to be thrown into question.** For some people, their entire worldview would need to be thrown into question. For if the information received from spirit guides is accurate, then spirit guides exist. And if they exist, this would prove the existence of the spirit world, the reality of life after death, and by extension, the existence of 'God'.

* * * * * * * * *

In our secular Western world, so entrenched in materialism (the belief that only *matter* exists), talk of the existence of God raises

Introduction

smirks, ridicule, and even contempt. While many Westerners have understandably rejected religions and religious dogmas due to the corruption and misdeeds of the religious institutions over the centuries – to say nothing of the nonsensical or contradictory statements in religious texts – **this has led many to reject spirituality and the existence of a Creator as well.** They have thrown out the baby with the bathwater, in a sense. Religions and spirituality are two distinct things. Just because I do not follow any specific religious organization does not mean that I do not believe in God.

Perhaps the real problem is our understanding of what God *is*. Although the majority of Westerners are atheists, their idea of 'God' is that of *"a white man with a white beard sitting on a cloud"* – an idea that comes from the very religions and religious imagery they have contempt for.

But what if 'God' is nothing like that? What if God is *pure thought*, pure *consciousness?* If one understands God as a "Supreme Intelligence", it may surprise you to know that scientists accidentally *proved* the existence of such a metaphysical entity as far back as the 1930s.

Quantum physicists, exploring the structure and workings of atoms – the infinitely small particles that make up all physical matter – proved that **all matter in the Universe is nothing but 'a unified field of energy'.** As they examined the fabric of matter itself, they discovered that in fact there is no real 'matter' in our physical Universe, though our senses make us *think* that matter is real (we *perceive* matter to be real, and solid). The particles that make up our physical reality are merely empty space with a pattern of energy running through them.

Furthermore, scientists discovered that these are not *separate* patterns of energy, but instead it is *a unified field of energy* that connects all things. All particles in the universe are part of *one* thing, and they are all therefore connected to each other. Some physicists say they can only compare this unified field of energy to a *'thought-wave'*. Well, *whose* thought-wave do you think it is? Is this the *Consciousness* or "God-Mind" that mystics have spoken of since the dawn of time? Are we a physical expression of the mind of God?

> *"The stream of knowledge is heading toward a non-mechanical reality; the universe begins to look more like a great THOUGHT than like a great machine. Mind no longer appears to be an accidental intruder into the realm of matter, we ought rather hail it as the creator and governor of the realm of matter."*
>
> Sir James Hopwood Jeans, English physicist (1877 – 1946)

Spooky Action at A Distance

The experiments conducted by quantum physicists gave rise to an even *more* baffling result: any time they attempted to measure the property of a particle – e.g. position, momentum, spin, polarization, etc. – their thoughts were found to *act* on that particle. In other words, scientists' intentions and thoughts were altering the physical properties of the atoms they were observing!

This implied that the scientists and the particles they were observing were somehow *connected,* and furthermore, those particles were exhibiting *intelligence* or 'consciousness'. Astoundingly, this transfer of information was occurring instantaneously, with no lapse of time, even if the particles being observed and the scientists performing the experiments were miles apart from each other. Albert Einstein would call this *"spooky action at a distance"*, and it flew in the face of conventional scientific thinking. And yet it would later be verified through further scientific experiments. The spiritual implications are astonishing.

According to Wikipedia:

> "It appears that one particle of an entangled pair "knows" what measurement has been performed on the other, and with what outcome, even though there is no known means for such information to be communicated between the particles, which at the time of measurement may be separated by arbitrarily large distances. Einstein and others considered such behaviour to be impossible, as **it violated the local realist view of causality** (in physics, the principle of locality states that an object is only directly influenced by its immediate surroundings; To exert an influence, something, such as a wave or particle, must travel through the space between the two points, to carry the influence. The Special Theory of Relativity limits the speed at which all such influences can travel to the speed of light. Therefore, the principle of locality implies that an event at one point cannot cause a simultaneous result at another point. In other words, information cannot travel faster than the speed of light). Einstein referred to it as "spooky action at a distance" and argued that the accepted formulation of quantum mechanics must therefore be incomplete. Later, however, **the counterintuitive predictions of quantum mechanics were verified experimentally**."

Science will not progress until *Consciousness* is factored into the equation. The thinking of the conventional scientific field has become sclerotic and turned into Scientific Dogma, akin to the

"Religious Dogma" they have been in opposition to since the 1600s. Much of what conventional scientists believe is wrong, though their ego would refuse to accept it.

Every particle in the Universe is connected to every other particle, always and instantaneously. Distance is no barrier. Everything is *connected*. But how is this possible?

> "Everything we call real is made of things that cannot be regarded as real. If quantum mechanics hasn't profoundly shocked you, you haven't understood it yet."
>
> Niels Bohr, Danish Physicist

The Origin of the Universe

The following quote may shed some light on why all particles that make up physical reality are *connected*. It also provides an interesting insight into the true nature of *God*, I feel.

In the channelled book *'Conversations With God'*, the author Neale Donald Walsch shares the following story on *where we come from*:

> "In the beginning, that which *Is*... is all there was, and there was *nothing else*. Yet *All That Is* could not know itself – because *All That Is* is all there was, and there was nothing else. And so, *All That Is*... was not. For in the absence of something else, All That Is, is *not*.
>
> Now *All That Is knew* it was all there was – but this was not enough, **for it could only know its utter**

magnificence *conceptually*, not *experientially*. Yet the *experience* of itself is that for which it longed, for it wanted to know what it *felt* like to be so magnificent. Still, this was impossible, because the very term "magnificent" is a relative term. *All That Is* could not know what it felt like to be magnificent unless *that which is not* showed up. In the absence of that which is not, that which IS, is *not*. Do you understand this?

[…] The All of Everything chose to know Itself *experientially*. This energy – this pure, unseen, unheard, unobserved, and therefore unknown-by-anyone-else energy – chose to experience itself as the utter magnificence It was. In order to do this, It realized it would have to use a reference point *within*. It reasoned, quite correctly, that any *portion* of Itself would necessarily have to be *less than the whole*, and that if It thus simply *divided* Itself into portions, each portion, being less than the whole, could look back on the rest of Itself and see magnificence.

And so *All That Is* divided Itself – becoming, in one glorious moment, that which is this, that which is that. For the first time, *this* and *that* existed, quite apart from each other. And still, both existed simultaneously. As did all that was *neither*. Thus, three elements suddenly existed: that which is *here*. That which is *there* and that which is neither here nor there – but which *must exist* for *here* and *there* to exist. […] Those who believe that God is All That Is *and* All That Is Not, are those whose understanding is correct.

Now in creating that which is "here" and that which is "there," God made it possible for God to know Itself. In the moment of this great explosion from within, God created relativity – the greatest gift God ever gave to Itself. Thus, relationship is the greatest gift God ever gave to you.

[Thoughts are energy. Thoughts have a vibrational frequency. Physical matter is condensed 'thought energy'. Pure thought started vibrating on itself at such speed that physical matter was created.] From the No-Thing thus sprang the Everything – a spiritual event entirely consistent, incidentally, with what your scientists call The Big Bang Theory.

As the elements of all raced forth, *time* was created, for a thing was first *here,* then it was *there* – and the period it took to get from here to there was measurable.

Just as the parts of Itself which are seen began to define themselves, "relative" to each other, so, too, did the parts which are unseen. God knew that for love to exist and to know itself as *pure love* – its exact opposite had to exist as well. So God voluntarily created the great polarity – the absolute opposite of love – everything that love is not – what is now called fear. In the moment fear existed, love could exist *as a thing that could be experienced.*

[…] In other words, not only was the physical universe thus created, but the metaphysical universe as well. The part of God which forms the second half of the Am/Not Am equation also exploded into an infinite number of units smaller than the whole. These energy units you would call spirits.

[…] **My divine purpose in dividing Me was to create sufficient parts of Me so that I could know Myself experientially.** There is only one way for the Creator to know Itself experientially as the Creator, and that is to create. And so I gave to each of the countless parts of Me (to all of My spirit children) the *same power to create* which I have as the whole.

This is what your religions mean when they say that you were created in the "image and likeness of God." This doesn't mean that our physical bodies look alike. It does mean that our essence is the same. We are composed of the same stuff. We ARE the "same stuff"! With all the same properties and abilities – including **the ability to create physical reality out of thin air.**"

> *"Look carefully at a rock, a tree, a table or your hand. Those objects are really just clouds of tiny particles held together by powerful electrical forces. Solid objects are mostly empty space."*
>
> Kelly Cline, Ph.D., professor of astronomy at Carroll College

Stewart Swerdlow, in his book *'True Blood, Blue Blood'*, states the following about the origin of our physical reality:

"In the beginning, God existed as a mind and nothing else. All there was, is, and ever will be, is mind. It has no idea where It came from. It only knows that It always existed and has no end. It allows for all thought and ideas to come to fruition somewhere within Itself. It allows any and all events to occur, <u>so in this way It knows Itself</u>.

It does not directly interfere with the personal lives of Its thought-creations. It does not have an agenda. Contrary to popular belief, It does not judge, interfere, or change anything that is already created. It allows for freewill of all creations within Itself. In this way, all possibilities unfold. Nothing is ever stopped from being. Humans may judge events and other beings as good or bad, positive or negative, but to the God-Mind, they are all simply pieces of Itself. The limited human mind cannot comprehend the enormity of creation.

There are many names for this overall intelligence. It is called God, God-Mind, All That Is, Universal Mind, Cosmic Mind, Cosmic Intelligence, Hyperspace, Supreme Being, The Almighty, among other names.

This initial supreme energy exists in a hyperspace state with controlling intelligence. **This is a state of being that is pure energy.** Here, there is instant transmission of thought and concept. The method of communication is via color, tone, and archetype symbol. This is the foundation of all creation.

In this light, as God-Mind thought about Itself and what It was, thought forms were created that self-perpetuated in creative thought. As this energy became self-aware, all the other forms or levels began to exist simultaneously. All levels of consciousness create the levels underneath them.

These thought forms created other thought forms, and so on, and so on. In this way, what is commonly referred to as Christ Consciousness and the Angelic Hierarchy were manifest.

Each manifestation, or level, is equal to every other. Where intelligence is focused gives a perspective to the consciousness. In actuality, all mind and soul-personalities exist at all levels simultaneously. However, lack of understanding and scope prevent full awareness of totality.

Eventually, a circle of creation is formed that feeds back to the original God-Mind, rather than a straight line as commonly thought. This is represented in the toroid shape.

Approximately 5 billion years ago, Angelic-like beings entered into this Milky Way galaxy and **attempted to experience life in a physical universe.** These Angelic beings who entered in to this physical plane quickly became both physical and non-physical simultaneously. [...] [Those] who stayed began remaining so long in the physical that they became trapped in the physical dimension. This is referred to as "the fall from grace" by many traditional religions. [...] Abandonment and feelings of isolation come from feeling abandoned from God Mind."

[...] "**Physical reality is the screen or the mirror that allows us to see/reflect our own thinking**. When you take responsibility for your thinking, your life gets much better. When you don't take responsibility for your thinking... it gets worse. [...] No one is a *victim*. No one is being punished. Everyone is creating their own life. WE are creating it. If you don't like the movie that is playing... you've got to change the FILM being projected onto the screen of your life. You've got to *think differently* so that there's a different movie playing. Your Thought is the film. The brain is the *projector*. Physical reality is the screen."

Time Is an Illusion of Physical Reality

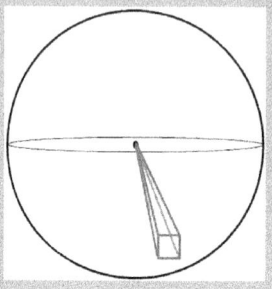

Imagine the Universe as being a hollow sphere, and our physical reality a film being projected on the surface of the sphere. Time would be the illusion someone would experience as they travel in a linear fashion along the surface of the sphere, from one point on the surface to another. But to an observer at the center of the sphere, they would be able to see point A and point B (the destination) at the same time. Perhaps it is from that vantage point that our spirit guides can 'see' what is coming down the pike... and help us correct our course.

The Universe is a Mental Construct

How can our solid world be made up of atoms, and yet we know that atoms are not solid? How can that be? There is no contradiction if you understand that we are all one Consciousness. **Atoms are not creating a solid world because the world isn't solid. It is a mental construct.** Our physical reality is merely an illusion... a virtual reality that allows for us to play out a game and experience life... for the purpose of self-expression and spiritual progress.

> **Are We Created From The Substance Of God?**
>
> "Quantum physicists now know that all subatomic particles such as protons, electrons, neutrons, quarks, and mesons are all actually *waves*. Your idea of having a solid physical body is an illusion of your senses. Your body is made up of nothing but electromagnetically resonant waves. Most of your body is empty space that contains minute fields of vibrating waves. You are a vibrating system. You are made of pure vibrating light waves, which physicists call *quanta*.
>
> [...] Think about this: If there is a Creator, what did that Being create the Universe from? There wasn't anything here before, so it must all have been created from the substance of the Creator Itself. So what are you? You are a tiny piece of the body of God."
>
> Dr. John Demartini, *"The Breakthrough Experience"*

Atheists Are Misinformed

I was very surprised, whilst doing my research, at how flimsy the arguments of atheists are. For example:

- ❏ *"God does not exist because I have never seen Him."* By 'Him' they mean the white man with a beard, on a cloud. This is kind of like a fish asking another fish *"Do you believe in this 'water' conspiracy they keep talking about?"* We ARE God... but atheists ask for *physical proof!* What do atheists expect exactly, a Larry King interview with

God on CNN? If *you* were *all physical matter across infinite Universes, all souls, and all the space in between...* would *you* bother showing up on a cloud to make a point?

- *"God does not exist because the Bible is wrong."*
  According to researcher Tony Bushby in his book *"The Bible Fraud"*, the oldest remaining bible in the world is the "Sinai Bible", and over 14,100 changes have been made compared to the Bibles presented today. Religions were subverted for political purposes a long time ago, to control the masses. Many religious dogmas have little to do with the truth of the spiritual world. Just because you don't believe in a specific *book or text* doesn't mean that God does not exist.

- *"God does not exist because if He did there would be no pain or suffering."* I guess they want the absence of free will, and the absence of responsibility for their own decisions.

- *"God does not exist because if He did, He would make us all KNOW that He exists."* Again, they want someone else to be responsible for what they believe, and they want the absence of free will.

- *"I was created by Nature, not by God, so God does not exist."* Who do you think created *nature?* Where do you think all the matter that makes up our Universe *comes from?* What do you think was there *before time began?* I find it astonishing that people don't ponder these questions, and just take scientific theories as fact.

It is high time humanity woke up to the fact that there is more to life than just physical reality.

Introduction

> **There's No God. Why? Because I Haven't Seen Him**
>
> *"I'm not religious. I don't know if there's a God. That's all I can say, honestly, is: "I don't know." Some people think that they know that there isn't. That's a weird thing to think you can know. "Yeah, there's no God." Are you sure? "Yeah, no, there's no God." How do you know? "Because I didn't see Him." There's a vast universe! You can see for about 100 yards, when there's not a building in the way! How could you possibly... Did you look EVERYWHERE? Did you look in the downstairs bathroom? Where did you look so far? "No, I didn't see Him yet." I haven't seen 12 Years a Slave yet, it doesn't mean it doesn't exist. I'm just waiting until it comes on cable!".*
>
> Louis CK, comedian, *Saturday Night Live*

We Come From The Mind of God

Where do we come from? It would seem that we come *from the mind of God*. Which, for a businessman and a hardened atheist such as myself was a very tough pill to swallow, when I first came to this realization all those years ago. If we are all part of *the mind of God*, psychic experiences may not be so bizarre after all. Quantum physics may even help explain psychic phenomena such as remote viewing, clairvoyance and ESP (extra-sensory perception): since the Universe consists of one singular Consciousness, and time is an illusion of our physical reality, why wouldn't certain gifted individuals be able to 'tune in' to the metaphysical world and even *to our future*?

* * * * * * * * *

This book contains psychic predictions and other insights into what our future holds, which I believe you will find particularly interesting.

In this book I have also included the predictions of economists, futurists, secret society insiders, and even people who claim to be channelling information from extra-terrestrial intelligences. I have included their statements because they correlate increasingly with the psychic predictions listed here.

> *"Reality is an illusion, albeit a persistent one."*
> Albert Einstein, German theoretical physicist

Why write this book now? Because a convergence is occurring. Altogether too many of these predictions are **coming true all around us**. Financial collapse, famine, civil unrest, and a war between Russia and the US are just some of the common themes. Maybe it doesn't hurt to take some precautions.

At the very least, it will be fascinating to see over the ensuing years how many of these predictions prove to be right. May all the predictions of war and strife be wrong, and may none of this come to pass. Or perhaps our world *does* need a period of purification before a "flowering of consciousness" and a "Golden Age" can occur on our planet, as some predict.

Introduction

With an open mind, a spirit of curiosity, and a solid pinch of salt… let's dive in.

CHAPTER 1

Prophecy of the Hopi Indian Elders

"Time evolves, and comes to a place where it renews again. There is first a purification time, then there is renewal time. We are getting very close to this time now.

We were told, we would see America come and go... In a sense **America is dying, from within**, because they've forgotten the instructions on how to live on Earth.

Everything is coming to a time where prophecy and man's inability to live on Earth in a spiritual way will come to a crossroad of great problems. It is the Hopi belief that **if you're not spiritually connected to the Earth and understand the spiritual reality of how to live on Earth**, it's likely you will not make it.

When Columbus came, that began what we term as the first world war. That was the true first world war when Columbus arrived. Because along with him came everybody from Europe. By the end of the 'Second' World War, we were, in America, only 800,000... from 60 million to eight hundred thousand. So, we were almost exterminated here in America...
Everything is spiritual, everything has a spirit. Everything was brought to you by the Creator, the one Creator. Some people call him God, some people call him

Buddha, some people call him Allah, some people call him other names, we call him Konkachila... grandfather.

We're here on Earth only a few winters, and then we go to the spirit world. The spirit world is more real than most of us believe. The spirit world is everything.

Over 95% of our body is water. And in order to stay healthy you've got to drink good water. When the European first came here, Columbus, we could drink out of any river. If the Europeans had lived the Indian way when they came, we'd still be drinking out of rivers, because water is sacred, the air is sacred.

Our DNA is made of the same DNA as the tree. The tree breathes what we exhale, when the tree exhales, we need what the tree exhales. So, we have a common destiny with the tree.

We are all from the Earth... and when the Earth, the water, the atmosphere is corrupted, then it will create its own reaction. The Mother is reacting. In the Hopi prophecy they say that the storms and the floods will become greater.

To me it's not a negative thing to know that there will be great changes. It's not negative, it's evolution. When you look at it as evolution, it's time, nothing stays the same."

"We always say, that [the ape] might be *your* ancestor but it's not *our* ancestor. He is a relative, but not our ancestor."

"You should learn how to plant something, that's the first connection. You should treat all things as spirit. Realize that We Are One family."

Chapter 1: Prophecy of the Hopi Indian Elders

"It's never something like the end, it's like life, there is no end to life."

Attributed to an unnamed Hopi elder

CHAPTER 2

Michael Griffiths' Prophetic Dreams of Russia and China Invading America, and California Sinking into the Pacific Ocean

Michael Griffiths is a New Zealand native who started experiencing a series of prophetic dreams in 2001. In these dreams he describes, among other things, seeing a woman being elected President of the United States; the destruction of a large part of New Zealand; and World War III erupting between the USA and Russia.

* * * * * * * * *

A Woman World Leader Will Emerge

> *"This is a dream I had in April 2009 about a woman global leader that would appear after Obama. A very evil world leader will come after Obama, a woman, and [in this dream] everyone seemed to be under a spell. [...] This dream may also refer to a more global leader of the U.N that controls the whole world, including America. Time will tell."*

This probably refers to Hillary Clinton, of course, though perhaps it describes a woman who has yet to appear prominently on the world stage.

* * * * * * * * *

Civil Unrest in America

"There is coming a time where leaving the US will become near impossible... because of a 'poisoning' that is going to take place there, and some other events... People will be trying to find a way out of large cities, but all the 'doors' are locked... I'm in a crowded street of an American city... some sort of bad event is taking place... I went into a shop, suddenly everyone was in a panic and trying to escape, but all the gates were shut. "There is another way out!" somebody shouted. I was forcefully kicking doors down... a sense of urgency to get out of this building, because of fire... [...] We were in the middle of this city... amongst crowds ... two large groups were walking towards each other. "Where is North?" I asked one person. "Don't go North, it's all poisoned or dead", he replied. I feel this is symbolizing an event coming to the United States...".

Dr. Patricia Green's Prophecy

Dr. Patricia Green is an evangelist and the founder of JOY Ministries. In a vision she received in 2015, she was shown a 100 ft. tsunami hitting the East Coast of the United States. She stated:

"There will be famine, drought, martial law, epidemic diseases, electric power cuts, dam breaks, earthquakes, huge hurricanes and economic hardship in the USA. Russia will invade and there will be nuclear bomb explosions..."

Chapter 2: Michael Griffiths' Prophetic Dreams

* * * * * * * * *

Russia and China Invade U.S.A after Atlantic Earthquake and Tsunami

"In 2001... I saw an ocean... I saw a US Navy destroyer, and it was attacked by two TU-22M Russian bombers. I saw Vladimir Putin appearing on TV and talking calmly about why it happened... It had to do with the US interfering with the Russian territory and interests..."

"In 2005... I saw this tsunami... I saw this underground navy base... and I heard this deep thundering voice say 'Nothing can stop us now!'. At this commander's voice, all these ships started to move, coming down this long concrete tunnel, and they all came out in this harbour...

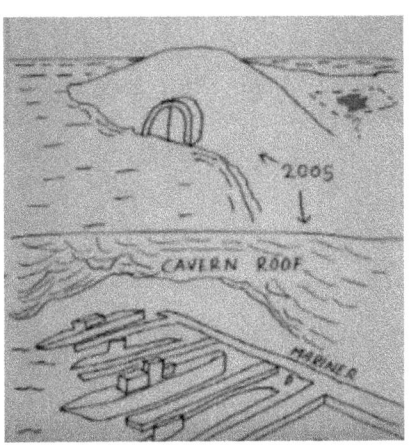

This military base is hidden underneath a mountain... it had to do with Russia or China... just before this dream I had a dream about a Russian navy sea battle, with Russian ships and submarines... so I assume it was part of the same narrative...

...Readers online told me I was describing the Chinese submarine base on Hainan Island...

... I believe there is a concerted effort against the US... there is going to be a major war between China, Russia, and America in the future.

God has shown me the slow demise of the United States through prophetic dreams and visions, and it is ultimately to bring a New World Order into existence... a One World Religion..."

"*I had a dream in 2007 about an Atlantic earthquake and tsunami which was followed by a Russian-Chinese military invasion. [In the dream] I was in an American city, with another person, going to a 'civil defense meeting'... [I saw] an earthquake, then a wave, and then an invasion from Russia and China...*"

"*I saw a missile being launched... I suspected it was Iranian... it struck a city and there was a huge explosion...* **I assumed it was an atomic weapon... the city I recognized it as Paris, I saw the Eiffel tower...** *[...] I saw a US frigate being struck by a missile in the Arabian Gulf... it was hit by surprise...*"

"*Another dream I had... was again about the Russians... and about Germany. I found myself among a crowd. We were in some sort of square. And there were a big number of troops. But they were very limited on our side. We had only 50,000 troops. The Russians and the Americans had a lot more. Some sort of coalition... The Europeans were trying to drive back the Russians... There had been two wedges of attack: The Southern part of Germany and the Eastern, Polish side of the country... A lot of people were hiding from the war in the mountains and in the wilderness... [...] I saw a major Russian invasion coming that some European leaders knew about... At the time of the events there is a stock market*

> *catastrophe and an earthquake that damages the region I live in, in New Zealand... these are the signposts to the season."*

> *"I saw the re-election of Vladimir Putin and then a future nuclear strike against America. I saw silos open, ICBM's in flight, cities in America on fire, mushroom clouds, and people surviving in the ruins and helping each other."*

Over and over again I have come across prophetic visions of World War III and a nuclear blast occurring *'in front of the Eiffel Tower'*... Is this mere coincidence or a grim omen of what is to come? My family on my mother's side is from Paris, and I have many friends and family members who live there. To my Parisian friends I say: *be warned!*

Russia Attacks Britain, Romania, Bulgaria

> *"86 MIG-29 jet fighters were involved against London... Russian jets... Yugoslavian people and Air Force were involved as well.... Romania and Bulgaria... were trying to stop the Russian advance... Soldiers from New Zealand were sent to Romania and Bulgaria... to stop the Russian advance."*

Riots Breaking Out in Europe

> *"This is a dream I had in 2008 showing riots breaking out across Europe... In particular I see France and the border with Belgium (orchestrated by two major powers...). The French president said something quite surprising: 'It doesn't matter, the country is going to be invaded anyway, in July...' and he was speaking of the Russians... <u>He knew that Russia was going to invade Europe</u> for some reason. The dream coincided with an earthquake in New Zealand, and a stock market crash."*

New Chinese Space Station: Future War with U.S.A

"...I saw clear details of a Chinese space station that was built solely for a future war against America, Russia was China's ally. It was above the earth, had massive capabilities. Real-time battlefield intel... linked systems... command and control... linked to helmet, guns, vehicles... They said they will use it for scientific reasons but I could see they will use it for a future war with US..."

How Russia Plans to Fight World War III

"...I saw the Russian military strategy on how to best deal with U.S/NATO. The dream shows how the Russians plan to defeat Western forces by playing the home advantage... letting the US come to [them] and fight them on Russian soil. It was a plan that had worked against Napoleon..."

[...] In my other dreams, I see Russia invade other countries with the intention of creating **a Russian-controlled Europe eventually**. *Also I have seen the destruction of U.S. cities at the hand of Russian ICBMs..."*

* * * * * * * * *

Comet Fragment Hits Earth

"...The second dream was about a comet or comet fragment that struck near the US East Coast. I saw the impact in slow motion...

In the dream, the news didn't want to report that there was a comet fragment that was going to hit the Earth... They were trying to keep it a secret. The guy from the news run away when I tried to talk to him. It was about 25 minutes before the comet hit. I saw the impact in slow motion. The key information was that they didn't want to say anything, to keep the people from worrying..."

In another vision, Michael Griffiths describes how two nuclear weapons deployed one after the other could save Earth from an incoming asteroid.

"[I saw] a very detailed dream of how the world tries to stop an incoming asteroid with a nuclear weapon and fails. The nuclear weapon was deployed ahead of the asteroid but when [the nuclear weapon blast] expanded to its maximum size, it <u>does</u> break it up into a lot of pieces but the rear of the asteroid survives. Their plan is not going to work. It needs to be through [two] simultaneous blasts. So you have the first blast, which breaks up the majority of the asteroid, and then another blast straight away, to break up the rear of the asteroid, because the rear of the asteroid will travel through the first blast. I think this is a warning."

* * * * * * * * *

New Zealand Destroyed: Tauranga, Waihi Beach, Wellington

"These dreams are about natural disasters that come upon the North Island of New Zealand, focused on Tauranga and Waihi Beach... I was shown a tsunami...

The first one hit Tauranga... I was walking down the street area and it looked like the ocean was raising in one place, a force was pushing it up, and the water was going to fall towards the coast. After that I heard yelling, screaming, [and saw] people, houses, cars taken by the waters..."

"The second one, sort of the same thing: the water raised up to the farmers' area in Waihi (100m elevation)... There was actually more than one wave... I see this associated with an earthquake...

The third dream focused on Waihi beach... same thing... the wave wiped everything out... earthquakes... I saw burning 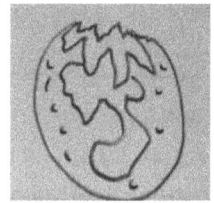 *clumps falling from the sky, probably from a volcanic event... The next day, after the tsunami, there were a lot of earthquakes... Australia was involved in helping organize the evacuation... Looking up, the moon looked as if it had been struck by something in space... the top part of the moon looked as if it had crumbled away, everyone seemed to be staring up at it..."*

"...I had a dream of a big earthquake that affected Wellington... one of the biggest quakes in the world... **one of the largest earthquakes in recorded history**... *Auckland was quite heavily damaged as well... I saw skyscrapers twisted and crumbling..."*

My wife and I love New Zealand, and I have many clients and readers there. In fact, we've been looking to buy a farm in New Zealand to establish a retreat center. The intuitive Stewart Swerdlow (see *Chapter 21* for his predictions) emailed me the following warning, though: *"I would not suggest living in New Zealand* **as the volcanoes there are about to blow..."**

* * * * * * * * *

Biological 'Zombie' Virus

"This is a scary prophetic dream I had in 2015 that is a warning of things to come in the U.S.A... I saw Obama and

the U.S. history being erased, as knowledge was being purposely removed from the coming generations…

…It was dark now and a full moon, actually there were 2 moons in the sky… A crowd joined us in our walk… At some point church bells could be heard, a funeral-like sound… and the people started to swing from left to right like zombies, half of them were normal, half were like 'zombies', affected by some virus…

My immediate interpretation was […] they are going to inflict the population with some sort of chemical weapon, this virus… and only half of the people will be infected…"

This dream by Michael Griffiths reminded me of a prophetic vision by a Norwegian man that goes by the name 'Gunnar Gunnar'. He stated in a video:

"I was standing in a room and I was placed in front of this flat screen TV and I saw the virus, [I saw] how it looked…

Next thing, I was still in the room and I saw a horse, a huge horse, and it started to become aggressive… I took its head and I tried to calm it but it become more and more violent, to the point where I had to escape the building…

I ran out and on the corridor there were people who were infected by the virus running after me. They were like zombies. As I got out of the building I saw a huge line of people [waiting for vaccines], and a stand where people were given vaccinations. The vaccine was mandatory…

In between their heads there were 'Coca Cola Zero' bottles and the word that came to my mind was: 'aspartame'. Not sure why… maybe because of 'lack of understanding', 'pollution of the brain', 'manipulation'…

> *I saw a woman with a four-year-old child in her arms, saying they were both infected... but I knew they weren't... she only said that to receive the vaccine... The child was going 'NO, no, no, we are NOT infected!' ...but she insisted, to get the vaccine... So I believe this is something created by men... it will make people turn into 'zombies'."*

The Greek Orthodox Elder, Joseph of Vatopedino, prophesied something similar in the 1970s. He described a war where men affected by this 'virus' would turn on each other in a murderous rage... (see *Chapter 18*).

* * * * * * * * *

California Falls into Pacific Ocean

> *"Last night, I had a dream of a large section of California falling into the ocean... I was [in a room] with high-ranking US military leaders... having a meeting... talking about Russia's military technological advancement... Su-34s... I could see a large Chinese military base that was all undercover and underground, it was an aircraft base. How it was situated... the aircraft on this base could all be refueled and re-armed underground, and they had a massive paved underground area where they could taxi to a high speed and then take off. A cross between a F35 and a Harrier... This could all happen within this building, so it could not be seen by satellite. These aircraft were waiting in single file to take off. The commander was growling at one junior officer because he didn't have his assets organized and he was going to be demoted..."*

> *"Then, I was back at the building with the US leaders, and we're overlooking the bay, in a nice setting... It felt like in this place there was a woman in charge of the military, airlines... she was high level. All of a sudden, there was an alarm... Like*

something bad had happened. Everyone ran off. She ran off. She went into a hall, and into a side-room. I went with her... We were watching an old CRT TV... we could see... 3D picture of the side of California... and a whole chunk of California had fallen into the Ocean..."

Many psychics and seers have prophesied the destruction of California (see *Chapter 17* for Joe Brandt's particularly detailed and harrowing vision of such an event). Once more, let us hope this never comes to pass, as California is an area of immense natural beauty, not to mention it is home to forty million souls.

I recommend you subscribe to Michael Griffiths' 'End Time Dreams' channel on YouTube, for his latest predictions.

* * * * * * * * *

Could the Russian and Chinese armies invade the USA and Europe? I wouldn't have believed it, but the following chapters do offer a lot of support to this shocking possibility. A 'zombie' virus may seem like the stuff of science fiction, but if World War III begins, considering we have had seven decades of scientific progress since the last global war, you can be certain that the weapons used will be unlike anything the world has ever seen.

CHAPTER 3

Rebecca Sterling's 1999 Vision of Martial Law in America

Rebecca Sterling is a former international banking professional from Atlanta, in the US. She claimed in 1999, at the age of 51, to have experienced a bizarre 'download' of information about the future. Her mind 'melded' with the memories of a woman named Mary-Beth, who had been alive in the US around 2016-2017. Rebecca could recall Mary-Beth's feelings and memories as if they were her own.

These 'future memories' were extremely alarming, to say the least. While she has not been willing to fully disclose all she saw, here are a few of her statements made in 1999:

> *"I saw a mixed-race man in the White House... The financial system's collapse will lead to lack... which will lead to riots across America. <u>The financial crisis will start because of derivatives</u>... Lack is coming... Lack of food, lack of water, lack of jobs, lack of money.... this will lead to riots. The communists will use this 'lack' as the match... to trigger the riots... I saw a lot of destruction and death in America.*

The Financial Collapse will help bring in a fascist system. Martial Law is declared by the time of the election. There won't be an election in 2016. You'll hear on the news: 'Since I can't guarantee a fair election... until the riots stop... we won't have an election'. Lots of horrible things start happening, as of September...

When the gas price reaches $4 a gallon... the carousel of industry will fall... [Note: the price of a gallon of gasoline was $0.58 in the US in 1999]. Industry sector after industry sector will fall. Then there's going to be an EMP (Electro Magnetic Pulse) attack above Kansas... it will take out all electronics.

Then the US gets hit by nuclear bombs. Mary-Beth and her family had to live in a basement for a few years...

People will kill each other... Neighbours will kill each other because they believe they have food left...

Jeremiah 50-51 (the destruction of Babylon) is really about the USA...

I saw the burning of America... the concentration camps that will come... They're going to call them 'Sanctuaries'. Our children are taken from us... The women are separated from the men... When there's no water, no food, you're going to RUN to these concentration camps! But the people that get out of line, or who complain, are shot on the spot...

When you are in these 'Sanctuaries' you are constantly being evaluated. If you don't say 'yes sir' on everything, you are taken away and decapitated by guillotine, as are thousands a day, and their bodies are used as food...

Chapter 3: Rebecca Sterling's 1999 Vision of Martial Law in America

The attitude of utter depression and blackness... You only live because of the anticipation of future pleasures... What do you do when there are no safe heavens, no future pleasures?"

> "We're going to set up these 'enemy prisoner-of-war' camps. I was asked to build one in downtown Las Vegas. Right on the railroad tracks. I show the contract in my book. They're building them all over the US. Bush signed an executive order... taking the old forts and army places that we shut down, to get those organized... to hold the so-called "dissidents". But what is a 'dissident'? We are going to enslave ourselves, because most people will still want to have food coming, so you're going to follow the line. You'll just walk yourself into your own prison camp."
>
> George Green, author of *Handbook for the New Paradigm*

* * * * * * * * *

Evangelist Glenda Jackson Predicts 2016 Election Will Be Cancelled

The evangelist and prophetess Glenda Underwood Jackson accurately predicted Barack Obama's first and second term in office, in the early 2000s. Her more recent prediction is altogether more chilling, and seems to confirm Rebecca Sterling's vision:

> *"It is going to be one of the worst elections we've ever had... They are going to be at each other's throats... It wouldn't shock me if*

someone got killed... but God showed me in a dream... Obama in the White House surrounded by Muslims and he said... 'I can't leave this White House... this is my destiny'... They asked, 'How can you stay on as president?' He replied, 'There is only one way... Martial Law!' They said... we know how to stir the trouble up... and you insert the Martial Law."

"Our economy is going to go down... There's going to be wars... food shortages... I believe that just before the election, Obama is going to declare Martial Law..."

"There is going to be disease that can't be cured, we will see more things that will come out... nation will rise up against nation, people turning against one another... Our enemies will come to our borders... people will lose their lives..."

* * * * * * * * * *

While race riots are currently rocking cities across America, let us hope that none of the predictions above will come to pass. The notion of 'concentration camps' once again appearing in the US – after the internment of Native Americans and Japanese people in the 1800s and 1900s – would be a particularly shocking development in our supposed 'Free Society'.

CHAPTER 4

Mena Lee Grebin's 1987 Vision of War and Famine in the USA

Mena Lee Grebin grew up in Chicago. In 1987, at the age of seven, she had a vivid vision in which she was told, *"A president will come out of Chicago who will destroy the freedom of this nation"* (Note: *Barack Obama started his political career in Chicago in 1985*).

In the vision, she saw herself as an adult in the Chicago apartment she grew up in. **On the TV there was chaos – scenes of riots, war, murder, and famine all over the news.** She went out on the street and saw that the wind was tearing up a newspaper whose headline read, *"American Freedom Has Been Stripped."* People were running past her and crying, *"The end is near. Run for your lives!"*

This was a very frightening supernatural vision for a seven-year-old and neither she nor her mother, who was also a prophet, fully understood it.

In 2012, this vision was brought back to her and it told her that **president Obama would be the last president** and lead the United States into the 'Tribulation' (*according to Christian eschatology, the Tribulation is a short period of time where the world will* *experience hardships, disasters, famine, war, pain, and suffering, which will wipe out more than 75% of all life on the earth before the 'Second Coming' takes place* - Wikipedia).

At the time of Obama's first election, Mena had seen in a vision the red horse of *Revelations*, **the second of the four horseman of the apocalypse, ride out**. *"Its rider was given power to take peace from the earth and to make men slay each other…"*. In that vision, she saw people in the US and around the world cheering the president's victory – especially many Muslims cheering and shooting off guns…

Towards the end of 2013 she began receiving an increasing number of visions. She was shown that **Russia would become a growing threat and that 'ISIS' would arise in the Middle East**, and she was shown the spirit behind it. In the spring of 2014 she heard *"death to finances"* and saw the black horse and the third horseman of the apocalypse ride out (the one that brings famine).

She was told that 'a recession within a recession' was coming to America. The stock market would crash, small businesses would fail and **those that depend on food stamps, welfare, Section 8 (housing benefits), and other government benefits would see them dry up**. She was shown a calendar with the months of September through December highlighted, meaning that this was when this vision would come to pass.

At that time the Lord told her, *"Those who are in me will be sustained, but not everyone who says they belong to me, belongs to me."* **She was told to begin to stock up on food for her family**, ministry, and others so that she could share what she had stored up during the coming time of need.

In April of 2015, an angel came to her and said, *"The countdown has begun."* She saw a digital clock showing 30 seconds before midnight. Three times her mother heard this phrase, *"Tell my children that time is running out."*

In a separate vision, she saw that **a massive earthquake registering 8.4 had hit California, leaving nothing but rubble**. She was told that many would die in this earthquake of such magnitude that it was felt in Arizona, Nevada and parts of Mexico. (Source: *'The Coming Storm and the Rising Ecclesia'* by Scott Flanagan)

CHAPTER 5

Barbara Marciniak's Prophecy of "a Flowering of Consciousness"

Barbara Marciniak claims to be channelling information from a spiritual collective that calls itself *"The Pleiadians"*. She is the author of *Bringers of the Dawn*. She made the following predictions in the 1990s and 2000s.

* * * * * * * * *

Technological Advancement Could Lead to Destruction

Barbara Marciniak writes:

> *"You are living in a post-technological world. The technological breakthroughs of the past 50 years are a small echo compared to the technological magnificence that has existed on this planet. In the past, innovation destroyed civilization. You must ask yourself: At what point does innovation lead to destruction?"*

In the passage above, she is referring to the Atlantean civilization, part of our history which has been erased from our History books.

* * * * * * * * *

City-Dwellers Will Become Sterile

"The toxicities and environmental factors make it too difficult to get pregnant. Some people will choose to have technological implants to improve themselves, by fusing with machines.

There will be those who will proceed into this technological future. And it's not going to be pretty. The body won't be able to handle these energies.

Maybe some of these 'machine riders' will be driven to go to the cities. But that's where the smart meters will be... [Editor's Note: smart meters are wireless and expose human beings to pulsed microwave radiation that can increase cancer rates].

The cities will be bartering points for jobs. Some people are hypersensitive to the electromagnetic radiation... Your city dwellers might become sterile.

Make sure you have a water supply, and that you can grow food. <u>Food is going to become a priority everywhere, because it's not going to travel around the world anymore</u>, it's going to become 'gridlocked'."

* * * * * * * * *

The Coming Financial Collapse

"The next few years (after 2013): Certainly you'll have big financial shakeup. Everyone will decelerate more. Everyone will get simpler; less waste, more creativity. Less money, more innovation. Less stuff on the shelves, but more stuff to eat in terms of nutritious food. You are moving back to a simpler time.

2013 to 2026 we call the Changeover Times. 2013 to 2017 are going to be VERY intense. Real deceleration, slowdown. Big stuff economically [financial meltdown], and you are in the window of possible 'earth changes'. Potential volcanic releases. The first 5 years will be intense.

2018 to 2027: that phase will bring a re-examining of what 'consciousness' is, and who HAS consciousness. And in the USA there will be the writing of a new Declaration of Independence, and a new Constitution for Humanity.

Your papers, your democracies... granted, they are noble, but you are dealing with entities that are using machines to take you over, to wipe out democracy, to create a belittling of you, a limiting of you. Don't fight the system. You can't argue with entities.

You have the power, you have the choice, of how you FEEL and how you THINK, and no one can take your imagination away from you... unless they tie you to a television, of course."

* * * * * * * * *

Worldwide Revolution Is Coming To Your Planet

"Worldwide revolution is coming. Political collapse all over the world. Chaos. But in order for something new to come out, things need to crumble. Things are not working. Why? Because people are so corrupt. The energies for the next few years will bring up some shocking truths about this planet. And it will bring worldwide revolution. And that revolution will play itself out in every manner you can imagine. Will people die during these revolutions? Yes. Will absolutely shocking technologies be used to attempt to control people? Yes. That is why you must work with the mind. The collective mind will eventually be able to shut down technologies that are harmful to you."

* * * * * * * * *

The Rise of Martial Law and the Police State

"Things are in place to completely control your lives. You will have regulations, mandates, surveillance, etc. that will come down so strong, beyond your wildest dreams... The countries of England and Australia are being used as test cases, to be applied to the masses.

These are acts of desperation... to control the flow of information, the exchange of energy, socialization, vibrations... These are attempts to halt the unfolding of spirituality, and of course to halt the loss of control that the non-physicals have over their physical puppets. They do not care about their physical puppets, they just jump onto the next one, within the same bloodline and organization, of course."

"Places like Detroit will see more control. The USA will be like Swiss cheese, great big holes throughout it. Louisiana, Florida..."

Marciniak is referring to lower astral entities that get 'attached' to some of the global leaders, to influence their decisions. This is, according to her, part of the ongoing spiritual battle raging on our planet between *'Good and Evil'.*

* * * * * * * * *

Nuclear War in The Middle East

"There will be a major nuclear war along the Euphrates... Iran possibly..."

This is an interesting prediction. A number of psychics have warned about the possibility of nuclear war between Israel and Iran. It was revealed this week by US General

Chapter 5: Barbara Marciniak's Prophecy of "a Flowering of Consciousness"

Colin Powell that Israel has 200 nuclear missiles... aimed at Iran.

* * * * * * * * *

Earth Will Only Have a Population of 1 Billion

"In the 1960s, the globalists recognized that there would be a point there wouldn't be enough food to feed everyone. They want it to go down to maximum 1 billion people. Six billion people have to leave the Earth...

It's going to be much more difficult to survive on Earth. Social programs will disappear. Those who don't produce legitimate value, won't live as long.

They tried genetic strands of diseases. Many nuclear plans have been stopped. It would be too messy, they would have to vacate Earth for a while... By 2028 we imagine that you are going to lose a few billion, naturally, even without a big cause. Billions of people are going to get sick. There aren't enough medical people around the world to treat all the people that are going to be sick.

People who will be able to afford medical treatment... <u>will go for treatment for one thing, and within 3 days they will come out with 5 diseases or more</u>... This is all symptomatic: The breakdown of the body, the breakdown of the system..."

"Everything you are doing about health is completely backward..."

"You are in an era where all that is not built out of solid integrity will simply dissolve, crumble, crash, burn, tumble, disappear. it simply cannot hold its shape anymore."

Many psychics and 'insiders' have warned about plans for 'depopulation'. It would appear that it was decided by our political leadership in the 1960s that it was critically important to lower the population of our planet, to preserve Nature and 'our way of life'.

* * * * * * * * *

You Will Start Seeing the Extra-terrestrials

"The next 17 years (2011 onwards) are for cleaning up, innovating, getting rid of the crooks and corruption. And you will start to meet the ETs. Or they will become more prevalent. Or there will be so many sightings and so many people having experiences, that they cannot be denied anymore. They could stage a phony invasion... using technologies with holographic projections into the heavens..."

* * * * * * * * *

Science Will Undergo a Revolution of Consciousness

"Today much of the world operates under a certain premise... Einstein's principles have been widely accepted for almost 100 years or so, when in actuality it has now been proved to some extent that the speed of light can be exceeded, and that the speed of light determines the limit of certain perceptions. If the speed of light changes, then your perceptions change. The things that you believe in as 'hardcore physics', what's to say that they are right?

Physics and Science are a result of pea-brained conscious mind ego thinking that you have discovered something... but there is no CONSCIOUSNESS factored into it. This is why science is on the verge of a massive revolution. Because they are starting to figure out that things are multiple, that this is a multiverse, that there are multiple realities, that you are multi-dimensional... and the laws that you have accepted as sacrosanct are absolutely not true.

If science keeps removing itself from spirituality, it won't go forward. Science must recognize that there is CONSCIOUSNESS in everything. That everything they are working with has INTELLIGENCE. Until then, they will keep creating more problems and they will get lost in a labyrinth of despair and insanity.

Tesla's work went underground, and now forms part of the secret science of the Soviet Union and the Western world. The Nazis were very interested in Tesla's work. And so was everyone else. Why? Because it opened up dimensional possibilities. It tapped into free energy. it allowed them to penetrate inside the Earth."

* * * * * * * * * *

The Truth About Our Planet's History Will Be Revealed

"There is huge suppression on this planet. Massive. About the truth, about what Earth is, about who occupies the Earth, and Earth's role in history...

France will rise in prominence, as a country that has sequestered a huge amount of information. Many things buried in the Pyrenees. Many things have happened in 'pre-history' in France that would completely change the outlook of how everybody thinks about what is going on, on this planet.

Malta has always been of very important strategic location to military and religious fanatics. Malta has openings into the earth that connect to the very ancient Atlantean underground networks.

Wars are produced to allow certain military, religious, secret societies to get into certain locations... More important than oil and natural resources... are historical artefacts, giant skeletons, devices, looking glasses, portable 'stargates'...

There's been a massive cover-up... A lot of people have lost their heads over the past 2,000 years, for those who dared to say... that the Piscean Illusion [the Age of Pisces] has been a bunch of nonsense." […] "This acceleration that is happening will crash people's beliefs. People will encounter truths that are very disturbing. And the global elite who have been pressing down these secrets... these truths cannot be pressed down anymore. Things will be shaken up, by truths that come out of the ground. And new structures will have to be built.

The Elite, the charges of the world... When these things start to mount, it will be shocking to many, many people. People will start to question, "Well, where does Jesus, where does Krishna, where does Allah etc. and all these Gods fit in, here?" There will be a disenchantment that comes along with religion, as hardcore data starts to be revealed.

Right now during drilling, mining etc. if anything is discovered, if anything anomalous is discovered, there is absolutely corporate rule: Close it down. Call certain people. Very often someone is 'disappeared' or 'suicided'.

In ancient times there were people of massive structure (Giants). But you relegate these stories to being childhood entertainment. Beings have walked the earth, and skeletal structures have been found, up to 100 feet in height. Skeletal structures have been found in Northern Africa, where the skeleton measured 35 feet in height. What do you suppose all the people with degrees, that are touting Mr Darwin's story are going to say, when this kind of evidence shows up? France is FULL of graveyards of 'chevaliers' (knights) who died in the 14th to 17th century, who were 15-20 footers... all

Chapter 5: Barbara Marciniak's Prophecy of "a Flowering of Consciousness"

before Darwin's decree, of course. This is a small example, to show you how the truth about your planet has been completely absconded."

"In the 1940s there were massive breakthroughs in understanding what is really happening. The Nazis were fixated on getting in touch with the Aryans, the 'supermen'. Who do you think these supermen were? Many of these clues are in the Middle East. And many things are being held onto now... Syria, Lebanon, Israel, Egypt, Iraq, Iran, Jordan... all of these countries... and France... they are sitting on 'secrets'...

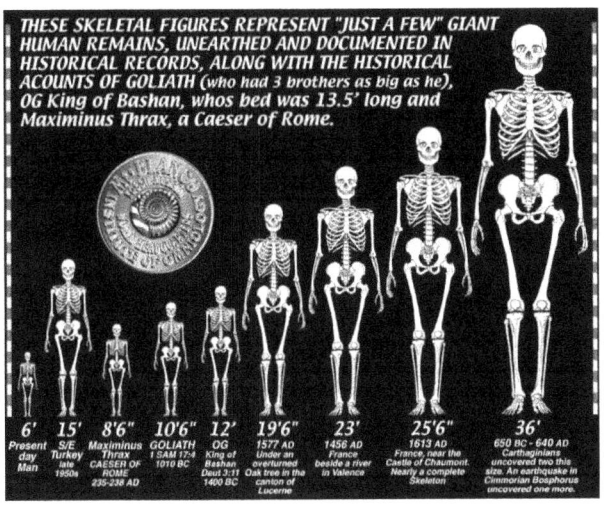

Why do you think that the US is building the largest embassy in the world, in Iraq? They are building this over the openings that will allow them to go down to and meet those beings inside the Earth. One of the biggest secrets of the earth... greatest mysteries... is the burgeoning technological Atlanteans who retreated to the inner earth, using their ancient tunnel system. It is one of the largest kept secrets. What is inside is starting to come out, in Iraq. That's what

the first war was about. Creatures. Beings. So this is about containment and location.

So we come to depleted Uranium. The same thing has happened in the Balkans. Things are starting to come out. Your society has created depleted Uranium, and poisoned areas that will be uninhabitable for hundreds of thousands of years."

In the passage above, Barbara Marciniak is talking about ancient Atlantis, stargates, and aliens who retreated to the inner earth during a period of cataclysmic changes on our planet's surface. According to her, the wars in Kuwait and in Yugoslavia were – in part – for the purpose of preventing these aliens from coming back to the surface of our planet. I realize that this information will put off many readers, because it clashes with their current belief system. But what if our planet's true history *has* indeed been suppressed by the ruling classes, for hundreds if not thousands of years? What if our history books were rewritten to comply with a certain agenda? **What if an advanced alien civilization *did* exist on our planet in our ancient past?** Psychics, Native Americans, the Incas and Mayans, the Egyptians, the Sumerians, the Zulu, and the Ancient Greeks all agree on this last part.

> He who controls the past controls the future. He who controls the present controls the past.
>
> George Orwell

* * * * * * * * *

Chapter 5: Barbara Marciniak's Prophecy of "a Flowering of Consciousness"

I visited the Greek island of Paros in 2014 with my friend Glyn, who happens to be a particularly gifted psychic. In fact, I devoted an entire chapter in one of my books to his story, where I refer to him as *"The Miracle Man."*

One night, as we were enjoying a glass of *ouzo* under the moonlight, by the seaside, Glyn made a series of predictions about the future of mankind. Although he asked me to keep these out of this book, I will mention the following prediction:

> *"Scriptures will be found, like the Dead Sea Scrolls, in Saudi Arabia or possibly Egypt, that are about the deals made with the Gods at the beginning of time… These deals have been broken, which is why things need to be cleansed, by an army of disciples."*

Edgar Cayce predicted in the early twentieth century that *"there will be three profound archaeological discoveries of a very ancient and important nature that will revolutionize the way we understand human origins, cosmology and religion…"*

Stewart Swerdlow stated in 2015: *"More biblical artefacts will be revealed, more history will be revealed. A lot of things are being discovered in Greece, other things in Rome, the valley in Egypt where they discovered one million mummies… Artefacts that will 'prove' certain biblical information [they] want you to believe..."*

It will be interesting to see if indeed, over the next few years, certain artefacts and writings will transform our understanding of our ancient past. Did the 'Gods' (an advanced alien civilization) really dwell among the humans, eons ago?

* * * * * * * * *

The Flowering Of Consciousness (2013 - 2027)

Barbara Marciniak goes on to say:

"The new era is predicated on a flowering of consciousness. Once the people of Earth receive these upgrades and they start to get awareness and they start to learn how to do these 'sit-ups in the mind' so to speak, there is going to be no stopping you. There's going to be what some call the Golden Age.

You will see more intelligence in people. More psychic abilities. People with psychic abilities with get 3-4 times more. The military is very interested in developing psychic military soldiers... moving objects with the mind.

The Rise of the healers: Abilities will develop. Systems will work with them to help people heal. The plant kingdom, it is essential that you focus on it. It will come into a much higher vibration, to help you. Not enough people say 'hello' to nature... You will eventually start talking to your plants, seeds, and flowers, to tell them what you need. Remember: nature supports you. So communicate with it."

* * * * * * * * *

As bizarre and 'out there' as the quotes in this chapter may seem to you, many of the predictions in the subsequent chapters of this book echo Barbara Marciniak's statements, regarding Martial Law, revolutions, and lack of food. Could a collapse of the financial system, an oil crisis, or the bankruptcy of container ship companies 'gridlock' the global food transportation system?

Chapter 5: Barbara Marciniak's Prophecy of "a Flowering of Consciousness"

My advice, for what it's worth: just in case, get out of the cities, have a secure water supply, and start growing your own food.

CHAPTER 6

Will Earth Have Fewer People?

An intriguing passage from the book *Journey of Souls*, by hypnotherapist and past-life regression therapist Michael Newton, points to the possibility that our planet will experience a severe depopulation in the next century or so. He explains that occasionally, his client not only relate back information about their past lives, but also share glimpses of their *future* lives, while under hypnosis. Michael Newton writes:

> "*The opposite of past life regression is 'post life progression', which enables some subjects to see snatches of the future as incomplete scenes. For instance,* **some [of my subjects] have told me Earth's population will be greatly reduced by the end of the twenty-second century**, *partially due to adverse soil and atmospheric changes. They also see people living in odd-looking domed buildings...*"

Could this imply that mass numbers of humanity will perish in the ensuing decades? Or will technology allow us to colonize other planets en masse? The following exchange with one of his clients, under hypnosis, is definitely intriguing:

> *Newton: "Do you think you will still be going to Earth when you near the end of your incarnations?"*

Client, under hypnosis: "*Ah… maybe no… there is another world besides Earth… but with Earth people… Earth will have fewer people… less crowded… it's not clear to me. I'm getting the impression there is colonization someplace else – it's not clear to me.*"

Ana Maria is an intuitive from Austria, whom I met at one of my live seminars. She sent me the following comment regarding depopulation, in an email recently:

"<u>*Approximately two thirds of Earth's population will be gone by next century…*</u> *not because the New World Order wants to, but because we all decided before time… therefore we clean up old karmic stuff, so that the souls can go home…*"

Chapter 6: Will Earth Have Fewer People?

"Human population growth is probably the single most serious long-term threat to survival... [...] As a boy I was made aware of [...] the need to adjust the "cull" to the size of the surplus population." – Preface to *Down to Earth* by Prince Philip, Duke of Edinburgh, 1988

"In the event that I am reincarnated, I would like to return as a deadly virus, in order to contribute something to solve overpopulation." – Prince Philip, Duke of Edinburgh quoted in *"Are You Ready for Our New Age Future?"* – Insiders Report – American Policy Center, December 1995

"It was explained to me by a Head of State, an elderly member of a European royal family, who was in her seventies, in my office... She said "You know... it's almost time for The Great Culling... the culling of the 'useless eaters' who are consuming our non-renewable natural resources..." – Dr. Rima E. Laibow, Medical Director of The Natural Solutions Foundation

"Depopulation should be the highest priority of U.S. foreign policy towards the Third World, because the US economy will require large and increasing amounts of minerals from abroad, especially from less developed countries." – Henry Kissinger, White House National Security Advisor, 1969

CHAPTER 7

Credo Mutwa Predicts Global Financial Collapse and World War III (1993)

Credo Mutwa is a Zulu Sangoma (shaman) from South Africa, and the only surviving keeper of the ancient knowledge of the Zulus. In 1993 he made the following prophetic statements, describing visions that had come to him while in trance.

* * * * * * * * *

World War III Will Arise in The Middle East

"In the very near future, <u>Islam will rise like a lion throughout the world</u>, and a new war will break out in the Middle East. A great Middle Eastern nation, I think it is Iran, will go on out to acquire nuclear power. Iran will buy terrible substances from China. Substances by which you can create atomic stations. Substances from which you can also create atomic weapons and other hideous weapons of that kind.

I see that there is a ship in the ocean. It is an old and ugly vessel which should have been sank or scrapped long ago. And it is taking some radioactive substance to Iran. One of the containers will overheat, and the ship will sink in the Indian Ocean. At first, the world will not be told about the sinking of this ship. Millions of fish start drifting dead and lifeless towards the beaches of India, East Africa, and Arabia. And the first inkling of this disaster that humanity will have will be when starving people in India and other countries nearby, they will eat these fish, and they too will die. And it will be only then that the world will be aware. People from the news will go to India to look into this disaster, and they will discover that many organizations were responsible for covering up this tragedy.

[…] There will be an outcry in the world. <u>The violence and the warfare will spread not only in the Middle East, but also throughout North Africa, as far away as Spain</u>. [The president] will unleash war and sanctions against Iran. He lays the bloody foundation for what must surely be the greatest religious war the world has ever seen, and that war is not far away into the future.

After president Clinton, there will come one other main president in the United States, who will rule for two terms. <u>After that president will come a female president</u> who will be a red-headed woman, a former actress, of French ancestry. This woman will become the ruler of Canada, the United States, and Central America, which three great masses of countries will come under one leadership. No longer will there be the United States of America, no longer will there be the dominion of Canada. The whole country will simply be called 'The American Federation'."

Note: The United States did indeed place an embargo on Iran and imposed sanctions (though these were lifted recently), and Iran is being accused of enriching Uranium for military purposes… Also worth mentioning is that Hillary Rodham Clinton is of French descent. Her daughter Chelsea Clinton is a red-head – I assume Hillary is as well, originally.

* * * * * * * * *

Chapter 7: Credo Mutwa Predicts Global Financial Collapse and World War III (1993)

A Powerful German Leader Will Unite Europe and Great Britain

"*Somewhere in the early years of the 21st century Europe will become one republic. She will fall under the shield of Germany, because a mighty ruler will emerge in Germany. In fact, he is already there. He will emerge, and he will rule Germany with a rod of iron. He will achieve with cold cunning what Hitler tried to achieve by brute force. And oddly enough, this brutal man, this second Hitler, will be hailed as the saviour of Europe, because he will strengthen the economies of the different states that form Europe, and they will call him the new Bismarck.*

[…] In the great upheaval that will shake the world in the next 50 years, strange and completely unexpected things are going to happen. It is all this upheaval in the British Royal family which <u>will cause the breakaway of Scotland as the United Kingdom disintegrates</u>, as Ulster separates, as Wales says farewell to Mother England, and becomes a state on its own, so will Canada, Australia, and New Zealand…

Australia will be torn away from the British Commonwealth by a man who will be enraged at the fact that the Commonwealth is becoming more and more dominated by non-white people. This man is already alive, but when his time comes, this man will be numbered as one of the greatest leaders that the British people has ever known. This man will confront the rising empires of Japan and China. A huge conglomerate of nations who will dominate the world with money. This man will confront these nations, and will not be afraid to send his armies against them.

By the middle of the 21st century I see the Union Jack as very different indeed. It will be just a red cross on a blue background. By the end of the 21st century, <u>Great Britain will have become part of EUROPE, a Republic ruled from Berlin</u>."

Germany is indeed at the head of Europe currently, due to the economic power of the country. Who will this German *"mighty ruler"* and *"second Hitler"* be? Could the "BREXIT" vote and the Scottish Independence vote in England be a sign of things to come?

* * * * * * * * *

Millions Will Succumb to a Man Who Will Be Seen as Their Saviour

"There is a young man. His eyes burn like those of a God. He wears the white turban of an Ayatollah. He is a man of Iran. He is the man who within the next twenty years or so will shake the world to its foundations. He is at present in his early twenties. He is a great admirer of Saddam Hussein, and at one time they once met.

This is the man many prophets have spoken about in the past. Some call him the Anti-Christ. In Africa they call him the Red Destroyer, the Moshiki Wadamu, the Lord of Blood. This is the man who is going to lead the rising hordes of Islam, whom future generations will call 'The Shining Sword of Allah', who is going to fight, shed blood and destroy cities, to restore once again the glory of the Caliphs. He will know himself as the Wahabu Al-Rashid… he will know himself as Al Timsah ["The Crocodile"].

It is this man who is standing in the shadows in this moment, who is going to carry on where his admired godfather Saddam Al-Hussein has left off.

I wish the leaders of the United States should be aware of the existence of this man. Because as they are humiliating and ill-treating the Muslims, they are only giving strength to this man, who is going to stand in a battle tank above the ruined cathedrals of

Chapter 7: Credo Mutwa Predicts Global Financial Collapse and World War III (1993)

> *Christendom in Greece, who is going to extend the influence of the lord Mohammed from the Western shores of India to the Rock Jabal al-Tariq (Gibraltar). And against his anger and against his might, not even the mightiest hydrogen bombs will prevail.*
>
> *In the next four to five years, Muslim fundamentalists will try to reclaim the entire empire, which was once held by the Saracens. They will claim Spain as their country. They will claim Portugal and all of North Africa.*
>
> *This dangerous movement will be based in the country of Morocco or Algeria. And one day a group of these men in a number of small boats will attack a beautiful cruise liner of Greek origin, and aboard her will die several people who are well known in the American film world. This attack will bring down the rage of the US and the United Nations upon the perpetrators. And one of these men will commit a serious outrage in a European city. <u>He will cause a tremendous explosion which could damage the Eiffel Tower.</u>"*

Is the Antichrist going to arise in Iran? Is there going to be a nuclear explosion in Paris? These are frightening scenarios to contemplate.

As I stated previously, many psychics have reported seeing visions of a nuclear explosion occurring in Paris, that 'melts away' the Eiffel Tower. This was also the plot of a Superman movie (terrorists place a nuclear bomb at the top of the Eiffel Tower), and it is an outcome seen in the video game *Command and Conquer: Red Alert*. <u>Paris also gets destroyed in the recent movies *G.I. Joe, Team America, Armageddon, Mars Attacks,* and *Independence Day*</u>. To my friends in Paris I say, once more: you may want to get the heck out of the city while you still can.

Prophecy 2017 – 2137

* * * * * * * * *

The Coming Financial Collapse Of The Western World

"People are going to lie and cheat. People are going to steal. People are going to exploit others like never before, all in the name of free enterprise and business. Very soon, I am shown, <u>there is going to be a serious money crisis in the Western world</u>. This crisis will affect first the US, with heavy loss of jobs, and the crash of the dollar. This will lead to similar situations in Europe, in Asia, and especially in Japan. [...] <u>They're going to do something to our money that will render us all to the level of beggars</u>."

In times of hyperinflation, currencies get devalued dramatically and render all the lower classes (those who do not own the productive assets) destitute. In Romania, when dictator Nicolae Ceausescu was executed in 1989, a family who would have diligently saved up enough money in the local currency to buy an apartment, would find themselves, overnight, able to only buy *a television set*.

> *"Based on the M1 money supplies of China, the Eurozone, and the US, and with 40% gold backing, the implied non-deflationary price of gold is $10,000 per ounce. [...] The increase in China's gold reserves is designed to give China gold parity with Russia, the United States, and the Eurozone, and to rebalance global gold reserves."*
>
> James Rickards, author of *The New Case for Gold*

Will the world's central banks print their way out of the Global Financial Crisis? Will they resort to "helicopter money" (i.e. throwing money to people out of helicopters, as suggested by central banker Ben Bernanke, to keep the economy going)? In

Chapter 7: Credo Mutwa Predicts Global Financial Collapse and World War III (1993)

Willem Middelkoop's book *The Big Reset* he states that the Central Banks' endgame is to "reset" the global financial system by revaluing Gold abruptly to at least $10,000 an ounce (everyone's currency will suddenly be worth ten times less…) and issuing a *new* currency backed by gold. Is this why China, India, and Russia are buying Gold at a furious pace?

According to hedge fund manager Kyle Bass, *"I look at Global M2 (money supply), being just under a hundred trillion. And the total amount of mined gold in world history is somewhere around seven trillion."* In other words, central banks have printed approximately 14 times more money than what the value of all the Gold mined in the world. Could this mean Gold should be priced at approximately 14 times its current level of $1300 an ounce? Will it reached $10,000 an ounce as predicted by Doug Casey (see chart below). Or will it drop to $400 an ounce, as predicted by economist Harry Dent? (see Appendix).

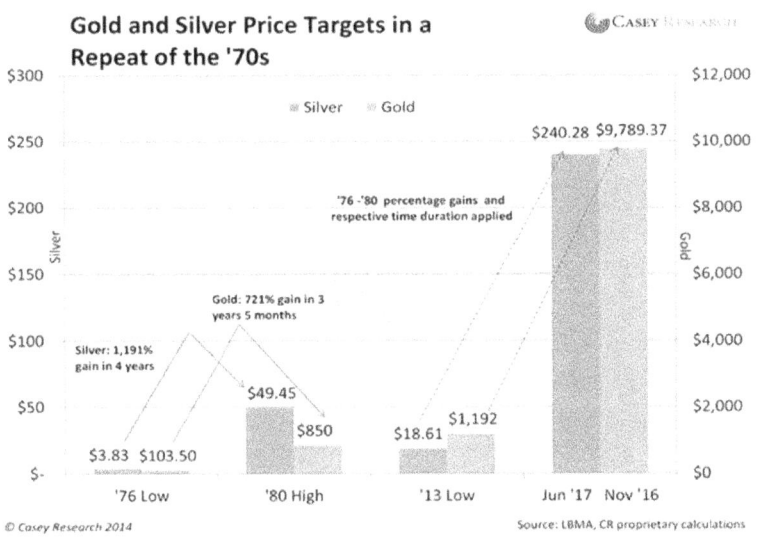

US congressman Ron Paul recently stated: *"The chaos that one day will ensue from our 35-year experiment with worldwide fiat money will require a return to money of real value. We will know that day is approaching when oil-producing countries demand gold, or its equivalent, for their oil rather than dollars or euros. The sooner the better."*

* * * * * * * * * *

China and Japan Will Dominate The World

Credo Mutwa goes on to reveal:

> *"As we go deeper and deeper into the womb of the future, for about fifty years, <u>the nations of China and Japan, Malaysia, and many islands in the Pacific, will dominate the world</u>. The former world powers will fade away. Japan will use the Chinese as the blade of her sword. And using this sword, of hard work, of technology, and of money, the nation of Bushido, Nihon, will take vengeance for what was done to her people in Hiroshima and Nagasaki.*
>
> *Japan will be joined by one nation, and I am surprised to name this nation: Israel. They will abandon Palestine. They will abandon Jerusalem, and carve a new nation of Israel in the Eastern border of Egypt. And there, Israel shall become part of the Federation of Middle Eastern countries."*

China and Japan may very well 'dominate the world' in the future, due to their combined economic and technological power. But seeing Israel ever abandon Jerusalem seems like an unlikely possibility. Or is it? The Canadian journalist Benjamin Fulford recently made this statement about Israel, based on information he allegedly received from Pentagon and CIA sources:

"Israel is now expected to become a Jewish autonomous zone within the restored Caliphate. Their attempt to malign moderate Islam by creating a fake radical Islamic ISIS boogey-man has failed."

* * * * * * * * *

The United Nations Will Crumble

"Very soon the United Nations will fall into pieces. In Europe, there will come a new league whose flag will be blue, with a large four-pointed star in its center. I see this flag waving with menace over Africa and the Middle East, and over India, and over Australia."

NATO flag

Could this be referring to the NATO flag? Or a new flag altogether?

* * * * * * * * *

The Descendants of Hitler Will Create Havoc In Europe

"Hitler did not die in 1945. Hitler escaped with a large group of scientists and military officers to South America. In my visions many years ago I saw two girls. These are the daughters of Adolf Hitler. There are Nazi groups in Europe who are aware that Hitler left children and grandchildren when he died. And these descendants of Adolf Hitler will create great havoc in the middle years of the 21st century."

Although our history books deny the fact, there are many eye-witness accounts of Hitler being seen in Argentina after the end of the war. Some researchers even believe that Angela Merkel is Hitler's granddaughter. Did a secret agreement exist between the

Allied and Axis forces to allow Hitler to escape, in exchange for ending the war?

Stewart Swerdlow states that part of the Nazi leadership survived the Second World War by escaping to an underground military base under the Antarctic ice. He predicts that in the next few years, *"the Fourth Reich will emerge, out of Antarctica."*

* * * * * * * * *

The AIDS Virus Was Created in a Laboratory

Finally, Credo Mutwa gives the following controversial account of how the AIDS virus began:

> *"I had a horrible dream.... a hideous vision... I was shown a laboratory somewhere in the United States of America... I was shown scientists of several countries, French, British, American and Canadian... all collaborating in a hideous experiment, which was* **to introduce a disease that would wipe out all armies,** *which would debilitate all populations in times of war.*
>
> *And one of these diseases is the thing we call 'AIDS'. AIDS is a man-made disease, created as a weapon of war. A weapon of war which proved so terrible that it had to be abandoned.*
>
> *They couldn't destroy the virus. They gave it to a firm of toxic waste disposals. But by that time a number of containers of this hideous disease had already been taken [to be] stored in a secret place. Someone suggested that some of them should be dumped in the North Sea, not far from the coast of Scandinavia. But others said no, they should be taken with other poisonous waste to Third World countries and buried there. A ship came from Europe, bearing these containers, and one of them had a fault. A sailor touched one of the yellow cylinders, and was contaminated by it through cuts in his hands.*

Chapter 7: Credo Mutwa Predicts Global Financial Collapse and World War III (1993)

When the ship arrived in West Africa, the cylinders were taken up aboard a truck. [...] The agreement had been that a hole should be dug very deep, but the official and his friends decided to pocket the money... they decided simply to dump the waste in an African lake, in a country called Cameroon. Some of the local villagers started becoming sick. And then, the disease spread into Central Africa.
In the very near future, people dying of AIDS will pose the greatest security threat that the Western World has ever seen.

The people who created AIDS have the effrontery to say that AIDS is a disease of African origin. That AIDS was created by God to put an end to homosexuality. They are telling us a blatant lie, that AIDS is incurable. It is curable. It can be cured, but not by drugs. In order to cure AIDS, sound, in various forms, must be used. If the sound is carefully calculated, the sound will be able to carefully destroy the AIDS virus inside the human being without endangering the human being at all."

As we saw in *Chapter 2*, a number of psychics have reported visions of a virus epidemic that turns people into an aggressive and violent "zombie-like" state, during a time of war... Will a terrifying new disease that can "wipe out all armies" be introduced in times of war?

* * * * * * * * *

Will an 'Anti-Christ' figure arise in Iran and lead "the rising hordes of Islam"? Will Islam "rise like a lion throughout the world"? Will the United Kingdom disintegrate? Will we see the financial collapse of the Western world? The way things are going, we might find out sooner than we think.

CHAPTER 8

The Prophecies of Sufi Master Naimatullah Shah Wali (1330 – 1431)

Naimatullah Shah Wali (1330 – 1431) was a Sufi Master and poet born in Aleppo, Syria. Here are a few of his astonishing prophecies, from 700 years ago:

> "There will be a war for 4 years on the Western continent (Europe). Inglistan (England) will cunningly win the war against Geem (Germany). This will be the first Great War. Mass murder will take place. 10.3 million lives will be lost. [Note: 11 million soldiers died, and 7 million civilians, during World War I].
>
> They will reach a truce agreement but this truce will not be a permanent one. Both the parties will silently manufacture weapons. Geem (Germany) and Aleph (England) will prepare for war.
>
> When Japan will fight against China, Christians will fight with each other.
>
> His first attack will be on France. British and Italians will also be in the state of war.

The Second Great war will start after 21 years. This will be more fierce and aggressive than the first war. Indians will also aid in this war. They will be unaware of the fact that this aid will be useless.

Weapons equal to the effect of lightening and of mass destructions will be manufactured by the famous scientists of that era.

Both the Alephs (Inglistan and America), Russia and China will join hands together and will attack Italia, Geem (Germany) and Second Geem (Japan).

This war will continue for about 6 years. It will be more bitter than the salty water and will be like a jungle crowded with wild beasts. [Note: World War II did indeed start 21 years after 1918, and lasted six years, from 1939 to 1945...]

After that, Christians will leave India [Note: India gained its independence from the British in 1947]. But before doing so, they will sow the seeds of wickedness (malice). India will be divided into two parts.

Sadness and Sorrow will result from the cunning and deceit. Turkish, Chinese and Iranians will unite together and they will conquer India. [Note: India has not been invaded by China and Iran... at least not yet].

<u>*The Third Great War will begin. Out of Two Alephs (England and America), one Aleph will be destroyed. 'Ra' (Russia) will attack the Aleph of the west.*</u>

The defeated 'Geem' (Germany or Japan) will become equal to (or unite with) the 'Ra' (Russia). Very dangerous, hellish weaponry of fire will be used.

'Ra' (Russia) will be destroyed by the anger and wrath of 'Seen' (China). Russia will save itself from China by cunning tricks. [Note: would China and Russia become allies during a possible Third World War, or will they go to war against one another?] Aleph (England or America) shall be destroyed to an extent that not a single dot of it will remain. Only its name and description will remain in the history books.

This is the divine punishment for them and they will be given the title of 'criminals'. These dishonest people ruined their lives. Finally they dwell in hell.

After that <u>the Denier Anti-Christ (Dajjal) will appear from the city of Asfahan</u> (Isfahan, Iran). Prophet Isa (Jesus/ Yesu/ Yeshua) will return to destroy the antichrist."

Source: Hafiz Muhammad *Sarwar Nizami*, April 1972.

Sunni Islamic Prophecies

The ISIS militant group currently operating in Syria and Iraq believes that we are living in the times of *'the End of Days'*, and point to Sunni Islamic prophecies as proof. The following timeline is taken from a book about the apocalypse, popular among jihadists.

Timeline of the Apocalypse:

1. Return of the prophetic caliphate

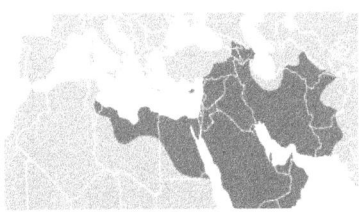

This relates to a geographic area that includes Egypt, northern Libya, Israel,

Lebanon, Syria, Iran, Iraq, Oman, Yemen, the United Arab Emirates, part of Eastern Turkey, as well as parts of Afghanistan, Turkmenistan, and Pakistan.

2. Mahdi appears in Mecca

According to Islamic tradition, the Mahdi is the prophesied redeemer of Islam who will rule for five, seven, nine, or nineteen years before the Day of Judgment, and will rid the world of evil; the Mahdi's tenure will coincide with the Second Coming of Jesus Christ (Isa), who is to assist the Mahdi against the Masih ad-Dajjal – the "false Messiah" or Antichrist.

3. Fight the armies sent by "Rome" in Dabiq, Syria

Has the Vatican instructed Western countries like France, England, Italy, and the US to send their armies to fight in Syria? French and US war planes have already bombed targets in Syria, and are planning ground troops, at the time of this writing.

4. Conquer Constantinople

Will Istanbul in Turkey fall to 'ISIS'? There have been three major terrorist attacks on Istanbul in the past eighteen months… or were these 'false flag' attacks?

5. Conquer City of Rome

A number of psychics have received visions of Rome being invaded by Islamists attacking by boats from Northern Africa…

6. Antichrist Appears in Iran

It is interesting to note the connection here to what Credo Mutwa prophesied in 1993, regarding the Antichrist arising in Iran, as well as Naimatullah Shah Wali's writings above.

7. Jesus Descends in Damascus

Will the long-awaited 'Second Coming of Christ' occur in war-torn Syria?

8. Gog and Magog Rampage

Gog and Magog may be references to 'America' and 'Russia'; the leader of Russia and Russia itself; or Satan and the Devil, depending on the various interpretations I have found.

9. Perfumed Wind Kills Muslims

Could this be an allusion to chemical warfare?

10. Sinners Face Cataclysm

This sounds similar to the Bible's *Judgment Day*. Let us hope we can avoid this "Third Great War" and prophesied cataclysm.

> "When The Jews Return To Zion, And A Comet Fills The Sky, And The Holy Roman Empire Rises, Then You And I Must Die. From The Eternal Sea He Rises, Creating Armies On Either Shore, Turning Man Against His Brother, Until Man Exists No More."
>
> *Father Brennan, "The Omen", 1976*

Prophecy 2017 – 2137

CHAPTER 9

Jamie Passmore's Prophetic Vision of World War III

Jamie Passmore is an English intuitive and clairvoyant. He started seeing visions and communicating with spirits at the age of six. When he was 19 years old, he was shown visions of a new world and possible future for our planet. These visions warned him of what was coming.

He was shown natural disasters, great floods, shortages of water and shortages of resources around the world. Huge areas of the USA will be flooded, as well as parts of the UK. The environment will get polluted through war, and parts of humanity will have to live in **biospheres**, to preserve and take care of our ecology. These biospheres could save humanity, he says, and he points to the 'Eden Project' in Cornwall as an example (*this reminds me of the Michael Newton client who reported – under hypnosis – seeing people in the future "living in odd-looking domed buildings"*).

Jamie goes on to say about his visions:

> "*I remember being shown living in tribal societies, in the Amazon, and how we will need to live like that again in the future... I was shown us living in peace... in a new community... In the future we*

won't need money, society will be based on a tribal system of sharing... I see us using alien technology and vehicles that work off of magnetism..."

The Eden Project in Cornwall, England

He was also shown how World War III would unfold, with Russia and China invading the West.

> **"I was shown Russia and China, 'red' soldiers, coming into the West..."**

I find it interesting that in the 2014 Tom Cruise movie *The Edge of Tomorrow*, the movie ends with the following news broadcast heard in the background:

> **"Russian and Chinese forces are marching across Europe without resistance."**

What do Hollywood 'insiders' know that they're not telling us?

Chapter 9: Jamie Passmore's Prophetic Vision of World War III

Jamie goes on to explain that it is up to us to avert this future.

> *"I was told that <u>these visions are being shown to us as a warning – it doesn't mean it is necessarily going to happen</u>. The balance is in our hands... Don't focus on war, destruction... focus on creating heaven in your own life... create an amazing life for you and your family... it's about how you live on a day to day basis... don't live in anger, hate... your vibrations on an individual level are affecting the entire planet and the entire galaxy. It's a warning on what we are doing on an individual level, to help bring about a higher vibration on our planet."*

> *"We are divine beings put here to evolve, we have a divine purpose for being here. We're not just here to drive cars and go to work... we're here to discover our true nature. More and more of us are going to wake up to the fact that we are angelic beings... we're not just human... More and more people are going to have these psychic experiences. More and more people are waking up to the effects of sugar... pharmaceutical drugs... We are waking up from the 'Matrix'."*
>
> — Jamie Passmore

CHAPTER 10

Edgar Cayce's Predicted World War III Would Arise in Syria and Turkey

The famed intuitive Edgar Cayce (1877 – 1945) made some startling predictions in the early 1900s, many of which came true. Here are a few of his predictions about our current era, as outlined by Kevin Williams of *www.near-death.com*.

* * * * * * * * *

The 'Battle of Armageddon' Will Begin in 1999

> *"Cayce predicted that the so-called 'Battle of Armageddon' would begin in 1999. [...] It will be a spiritual struggle between the 'higher forces of light' and 'lower forces of darkness' for 1000 years of Earth time. The reason for this struggle is to prevent souls from lower afterlife realms from reincarnating to Earth. By preventing souls from the lower afterlife realms from reincarnating to Earth, only enlightened souls will be permitted to reincarnate. <u>The result will be 1000 years of building a world of peace and enlightenment.</u>"*

* * * * * * * * *

World War III Will Arise in Syria and Turkey

*"Cayce foresaw the possibility of a third world war. He spoke of strife arising near the Davis Straits, and **in Libya, in Egypt, in Ankara, and in Syria**; through the straits around those areas above Australia, in the Indian Ocean and the Persian Gulf. […] Cayce often maintained that humanity would soon experience a 'day of reckoning'."*

* * * * * * * * *

Major Archaeological Discoveries Will Transform Our Views on Human Origins

"Cayce predicted that there will be three profound archaeological discoveries of a very ancient and important nature that will revolutionize the way we understand human origins, cosmology and religion. Cayce stated that this will occur when humanity reaches a higher level of spirituality. The three repositories mentioned are in Egypt (near the Great Pyramid), the Bimini area (where the possible portion of Atlantis has already been discovered), and the Yucatan."

* * * * * * * * *

America's West Coast Will Be Destroyed

"The widespread destruction in Los Angeles and San Francisco as well as in many portions of the West Coast will occur. Earth changes will occur in the central portion of the United States as well. Near-Death Experience researcher Dr. Kenneth Ring discovered that many near-death accounts he was studying foretell future Earth changes such as earthquakes, volcanoes, a pole shift, strange weather patterns, droughts, famines, tidal waves and a <u>new social order followed by a golden age</u>."

Chapter 10: Edgar Cayce's Predicted World War III Would Arise in Syria and Turkey

* * * * * * * * *

Northern Europe and Japan Will Be Submerged

Cayce also foresees the ocean level rising significantly:

> "The Earth will be broken up in the western portion of America. The greater portion of Japan must go into the sea. The upper portion of Europe will be changed as in the twinkling of an eye. Land will appear off the east coast of America."

* * * * * * * * *

Tremendous Earth Changes, Followed By New Era Of Peace And Enlightenment

Cayce foresaw a new era of enlightenment and peace for humanity in the future. Cayce states:

> "A new order of conditions is to arise; there must be a purging in high places as well as low; and there must be the greater consideration of the individual, so that each soul being his brother's keeper. Then certain circumstances will arise in the political, the economic, and whole relationships to which a levelling will occur or a greater comprehension of the need for it."

> "[Edgar Cayce] described a new era of enlightenment and peace when divinity within humans would be manifested on the Earth. But before this "kingdom of God" would rule the world, Cayce foresaw world events that can only be described as apocalyptic; **a period of purification involving natural disasters** that will dramatically alter the surface of the Earth, **wars, economic collapse, and socio-political unrest.** Cayce believed that <u>these horrible future events could be averted if humanity changed its behaviour.</u> And this is the purpose for giving prophecies – to warn people to change so that the prophecies

won't happen. Cayce envisioned that a time would come when all individuals would realize their responsibility toward one another a realization that would change the thought of humanity."

* * * * * * * *

Cayce Foresaw His Next Incarnation
Cayce once had a prophetic dream involving an event in his next incarnation on Earth. He wrote:

"I had been born again in 2100 A.D. in Nebraska. The sea apparently covered all of the western part of the country, as the city where I lived was on the coast. The family name was a strange one. At an early age as a child I declared myself to be Edgar Cayce who had lived 200 years before. [...] Water covered part of Alabama. Norfolk, Virginia, had become an immense seaport. New York had been destroyed either by war or an immense earthquake and was being rebuilt. Industries were scattered over the countryside. Most of the houses were built of glass."

* * * * * * * * * *

Cayce himself stated that the future is not fixed and that human free will makes virtually everything possible. Let us hope that there is still time to change our course.

Chapter 10: Edgar Cayce's Predicted World War III Would Arise in Syria and Turkey

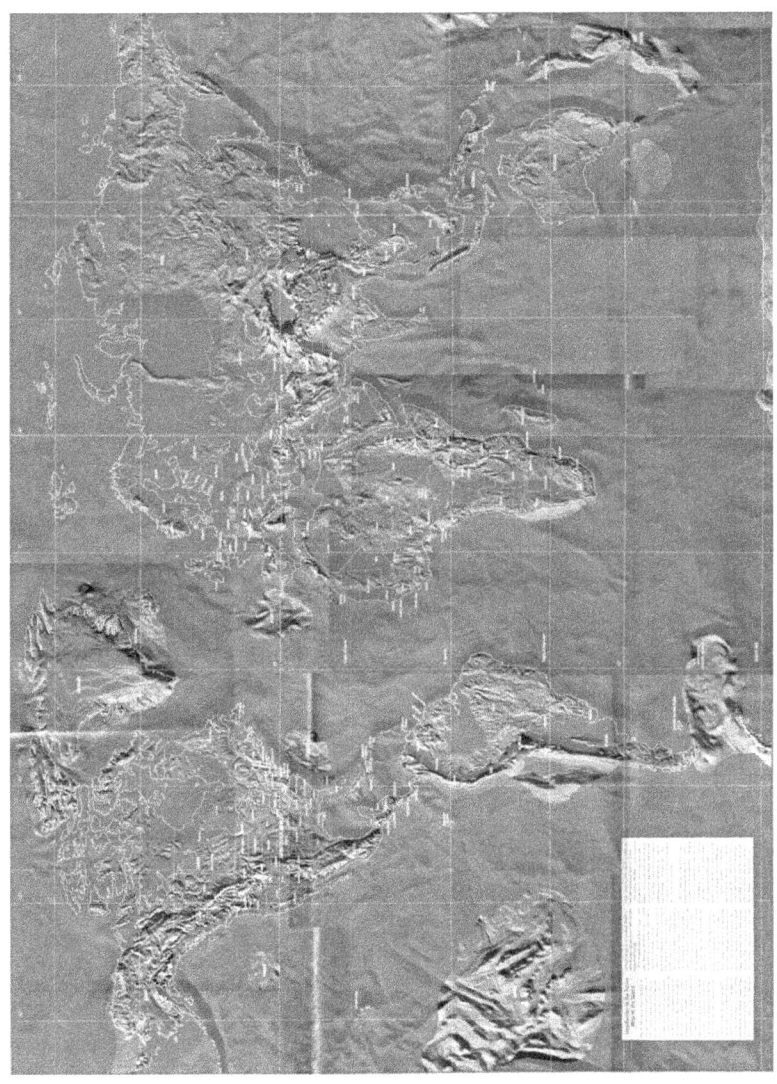

Gordon-Michael Scallion's Future Map of Earth, after the 'Earth Changes'

CHAPTER 11

Raymond Aguilera's Prophetic Visions of the End of America and World War III

Raymond Aguilera is an artist based in El Sobrante, California. After an emotionally turbulent time in his life, he went into a church to pray. Soon thereafter, in 1990, he began seeing visions of future events. He has received more than 2000 prophetic visions to date, many of which refer to nuclear war occurring on our planet. The following visions are just a small sample.

* * * * * * * * *

Nuclear War is Coming

> "*Russia will reassemble, reorganize. <u>The False Prophet will be risen from the Middle East, and he will unite with the Beast at the appointed hour in time</u>. This False Prophet from the Middle East, is going to use the Power of Satan to deceive. He is going to create Miracles. He is going to do things that you're going to consider wondrous, great.*"

Does the passage above refer to Russia uniting militarily with Iran? This vision is also reminiscent of the predictions by Credo Mutwa and Naimatullah Shah Wali, regarding the Antichrist arising in Iran…

* * * * * * * * *

"Then the Lord said: 'The beginning of the end will begin when the oil stops'."

If war were to disrupt the global oil production industry, or if the global system of oil transportation were to stop (oil tankers, pipelines, etc), industry would come to a halt, millions would be out of a job, trucks would not run, supermarket shelves would be empty within a week, and millions of homes would be without heating. Are interconnected world is quite fragile, in that regard.

* * * * * * * * *

"Show Me Moscow and I will show you the pit of hell. For the things in Moscow are going to change for the worse. For the reorganization of Russia will begin. It will be violent. It will be complete. For the devil is going to come from underneath all the rocks, from the sewers, from the alleys, and he is going to create an uprising. For the hammer and the sickle will be used on the people."

The hammer and the sickle refers to Communism. Are things in Russia about to take a turn for the worse?

* * * * * * * * *

The Lord said, "Holland will be the first of the Beast". The Lord said, "Texas will be the second of the Beast." […] "The Province of Bolivia will become a desolate land, for the arm of the beast, the angels of the beast, will destroy and annihilate the Province of Bolivia with a powerful hand."

Chapter 11: Raymond Aguilera's Prophetic Visions of the End of America and World War III

> *"The last big War to be fought will happen in your lifetime. So be prepared, be strong, practice the Word of God in your everyday living. Practice the rules, the regulations that are stated in the Bible. Look to Jesus Christ of Nazareth, look to the Holy Spirit to guide you, look to Me to listen to your prayers, for the day of the Beast is here. For the number of the Beast will be implemented on the weak, on the Sinful. DO NOT, I'll repeat it again! DO NOT TAKE THE SIGN OF THE BEAST. For if you do, you will not find Salvation. I'll state it again. DO NOT TAKE THE SIGN OF THE BEAST. No matter how hard it gets, no matter how easy it gets, if you value, and I mean, if you value your future, do not take the sign of the beast, for you will be condemned to the valley of death for eternity."*

Many have forewarned that a new cashless society will require a chip being implanted in the forehead or in the arm, to allow for buying and selling things 'safely'.

* * * * * * * * *

> *"...all that you believed of the wars is <u>going to begin in North Korea</u>... For they are going to move toward the south. Yes! They are going to move with hunger, with the hunger of the force that they have. For they have arrived at the point that they want to do something, with their power, with their soldiers, with all that is of the devil."*

Some seers have predicted that Word War III will begin in Iran or Syria, while some have stated that North Korea could be the trigger point.

> *"<u>I see a nuclear explosion go off in front of the Eiffel Tower and the Tower melted like a candle.</u> [...] During prayer in church I saw the Golden Gate Bridge [in San Francisco] and a nuclear explosion went off near the Bridge. ...I saw another nuclear explosion. I saw*

the one first in Paris, then I saw one, another one someplace else. I guess there is going to be two. The second one I saw, the Lord revealed that it was going to be in Dunkirk."

A nuclear explosion in Paris is a theme that comes up again and again…

"There are going to be explosions in the Big Capitals, in the Big Cities, all over the World. There is going to be a Police Force that will have no law, only the law of the Antichrist, which is the law of Satan. He is going to develop a Kingdom, a source of Power where he can control what People buy, what they sell, who is living in their house, who and where their family members are, what they do for a living, where they go to church, where they don't go to church. He's going to have that kind of control. Then he is going to implement the Seal which is going to be placed on the foreheads of his puppets; which He'll control and manipulate to do his bidding. If you value your Spiritual Life do not take the Seal of the Beast."

"<u>The heartland of Europe will be destroyed beyond repair</u>…"

"… I kept seeing in the spirit nuclear explosions going off in Africa, South America, Europe, China, United States, and Canada. These nuclear explosions were going off all over the place…"

"…The Lord showed me a reddish brown soft leather suitcase the kind you take on airplanes. Then the Lord said, 'Inside the suitcase there is a nuclear device'."

"… the Lord showed me a nuclear explosion as we approached Rotterdam (Holland). I saw three nuclear bombs go off in Rotterdam…"

"Holland will be split in two pieces".

Chapter 11: Raymond Aguilera's Prophetic Visions of the End of America and World War III

> "...Somehow I could see the upper atmosphere of the earth. I could see that these destroying missiles were coming from what looked like circling satellites. As I looked at these attacking missiles come down, the ground forces tried to shoot them down, and by shooting up larger and fatter looking missiles into the atmosphere. All of this looked like there was some kind of war going on..."

* * * * * * * * *

The End of America

> "I had a vision of nine figures surrounding Uncle Sam... and the nine figures knocked Uncle Sam down to the ground, and he stayed there. [...] Then the Lord said, 'Japan is one of the ten horns (kingdoms) of the Antichrist from the Book of Revelations. Japan will unite with the other nine and attack Babylon in one hour'."

> "... the Lord said, 'When Bill Gates falls, will begin the beginning of the end'."

> "<u>The country of Canada is going to become stronger</u>, for all things of the United States are filthy. That's why the country of Canada is going to become stronger. For they are not going to want the filthy things of the United States. For the people of Canada still have more people with a clean mind than the manner of the devil. And they are not going to want all the filth of the south; of the United States; to go north into their country. Yes! They are going to close the roads. It's going to be harder to enter Canada for the filth of the United States. Mark it on your calendar. It has arrived. The days the roads going to Canada from the United States are going to close little by little."

* * * * * * * * *

Famine and Martial Law

"Here comes the day that they are going to kill the old people too… and the sick ones and the ones who study the Bible. All of them, they are going to gather and they are going to kill them, like they do animals. […] For people are going to eat rats, dogs, and cats. And they are going to eat everything that is filthy…"

"You have to tell people to <u>buy food, and save water</u>. For here comes the whirlwind. The whirlwind is going to come, and hit the United States."

"You have to look for a place to hide! With food and water. For there is going to be a day that there won't be food or water, only the bullets of the soldiers, of the man who thinks he is god. And he is not going to care who he is going to kill, and there are going to be millions that are going to die. …They have to hide, with food, with water, with clothes. Yes, with blankets for its going to be cold, for the WORLD is going to become cold."

* * * * * * * * *

A Virus Will Spread Around the World

"…The Lord is showing me a virus. It starts off with the shape of a flower, and the Lord is telling me that it is going to go all over the world."

As we've seen previously, many psychics have predicted that a deadly virus will spread around the world and kill millions of people. Avoid the cities, if you can.

* * * * * * * * *

Islam Will Be the Way Of The Future

"Islam will be the way of the future. The antichrist, the false prophet will eat Islam, will digest it, adore it, will live it. Remember My Words. Islam will be the way of the devil, will be the way of the antichrist. Islam. Remember the Star of David. The Star of David will appear, when the false prophet becomes the head of the church of Islam."

This is reminiscent of Credo Mutwa's pronouncement, seen in Chapter 7, of *"Islam rising like a lion throughout the world…"*

* * * * * * * * *

Monarch Assassinated In London

"Yes Ray, **the hour will come when the monarch is assassinated in the streets of London.** *On the Day that will mark his Coronation. For the Beast has planned, and executed this assassination from the beginning."*

* * * * * * * * *

California Earthquake and Flood

"The earthquake that is going to hit the United States and the earthquake of California. It has arrived, the Force of God. It has arrived, 'The End of everything that is filthy in California'."

"…He was showing me the end of this particular area possibly by an explosion of Mt. Shasta [in California] which will destroy an area in 7 states…"

"I had the same vision about two years ago: Where these mountains of water hit a valley filled with suburban houses and totally

destroyed everything. I can still see these mountains of water as if it was yesterday. This vivid vision did not have a location, but today the Lord revealed that it was the San Francisco Bay Area. The massive water hit Concord, California, in the county of Contra Costa, all the way to the town of Byron, some sixty miles inland. All that could be seen afterwards were the mountain peaks of Mt. Diablo and Mt. Tamalpais. They looked like two islands in the middle of the ocean."

"During prayer <u>I had a vision of water rising over the San Francisco Golden Gate Bridge and totally covering it</u>. I couldn't tell if the Golden Gate Bridge was sinking or if the water was rising over it, but as I watched, it disappeared and went under the water. The water covered the Golden Gate Bridge slowly almost like it sank into the San Francisco Bay. I couldn't see a large wave or any great disturbance in the water. It just slowly went under the water. [...] People were deserting the city of Oakland in great numbers..."

* * * * * * * * *

Asteroid Colliding with Earth and Earth Changes

"...I could see the planet Earth. Out of nowhere a large hot rock appeared. I could see the black outer surface with its red inner core glowing bright red. As the black rock hit the planet Earth it bounced on the countries, continents, and the state of Texas that I had seen earlier in the vision. In the next image, I could see the Earth as you see it from outer space. It looked so beautiful with its white clouds and blue green water, I could even see the weather patterns. I don't know from where Jesus Christ came from, but He was standing next to me as I watched the planet Earth. Then all of a sudden the planet disappeared and all I could see was black space. I remember I argued with Christ because the planet just vanished into nothing. He showed me the planet two more times and each time it disappeared into nothing. This really upset me for I kept *arguing with Him. Then out of nowhere a new planet appeared, but this planet was three to four times bigger than the planet Earth. It had a bright white light on the outside of it with a dark center."*

"Yes, the things of the world will become cold. Buy yourself blankets. Buy yourself firewood. The places that were hot are going to become cold. Everything is going to become different, all the climate of the world is going to change."

"Open your faucet and it will be dry. For there will be a day... when your rivers will dry up... when the valleys will be scorched... The ground will crack for the lack of water. Your throat will blister. Your lips will blister for the lack of water."

"The ice of the north will begin to move, which will cause the water of the oceans to shift. The land that's near the water will be under water. For the waves that will hit the continent are going to be larger than the mountains you have on the Planet. Look at the water! Look at the wonders and signs that are going to befall this Planet. Look at the ice of the north. For it will begin to move as the axis of the Earth shifts. When the temperature of the Planet rises, the ice of the north will melt and will begin to move."

"The climates of the planet are going to change. The tides of the ocean are going to go up and down… higher than mountains and lower than the valleys that you have on the planet. The ocean is going to rise; it is going to go down. All the ice in the North and the South are going to move. They're not just going to move slowly…. They are going to ram continents with such force you'd never believe such things could happen. Remember the violent things that are going to happen to this planet. …Winter will not be winter. Summer will not be summer. Fall will not be fall. From all the corners of the earth, from the North, from the South, from the East, from the West, everything will be turned upside down. The climates are going to change. Some of you are not going to have houses

because of that climate ...the weather...the storms. The hurricanes, tornadoes..."

"Hear Me, My Sons and My Daughters. This is your God. He is going to burn the world with a star, with a piece of a star. It is going to burn the world, **in a thousand and so many years. It is going to come.** *[...] There are going to be many earthquakes, many storms, many signs, the ocean is going to move up and down. The ice of the oceans is going to move. The ice of the North and the South."*

Does this mean that we are at least a thousand years away from these cataclysmic 'Earth Changes'? Or will they occur in our lifetime?

* * * * * * * * *

Once again, let's pray that none of these apocalyptic scenarios come to pass.

CHAPTER 12

Terry Bennett's Vision of Anarchy and Lawlessness in the US

In 2001, prophetic minister Terry Bennett was shown a 21-year timeframe, divided into three periods of seven years each, starting in 2008 and ending in 2028. The first period would be about *economics*, the second one would be *political*, and the third one would see a *religious* system being added to the new economic and governmental political systems.

> *"In December 2001 the angel came to me over a series of three or four days. During that time, he spoke to me about these coming years beginning in 2008, which he called the beginning of birth pangs, not just in our nation, but throughout the nations… […] What I saw was the stock market in the United States of America drop below 500 points. That is not 5,000 points. It is 500 points. [Note: The US stock market is currently at 18,491 points]. The angel told me, 'Weep for what is coming upon your nation'. The angel made it very clear to me concerning four nations. He said to me: 'I want you to watch four nations. They are sign-posts for what is going to happen. The four nations are Greece, Italy, Spain, and France'."*

"...These three seven-year periods are laying the foundation for the Antichrist world system. That does not mean the Antichrist is coming in 2028, but it does mean certain foundations are being laid. Not all nations will adopt all three of these systems. Some nations will adopt one or two while others will adopt all three. Each nation made its own decision. The intercessors will also determine to what degree the nations will adopt these evil systems and to what degree the nations will become refuge nations. There will be many nations that will refuse to adopt these evil systems..."

In 2013, Bennett made the following predictions:

"The USA Government WILL fall. <u>Obama will use the racial card to ignite widespread protests in many cities</u>. There will be a governmental takeover from within. <u>Chaos, anarchy and lawlessness will ensue</u>. The government will deteriorate and then disintegrate. There will be a fractionalized government in the USA. Great civil unrest and conflict will rage, millions will be lost. ...this nation implodes upon itself. The U.N. will seek to help/intervene. <u>Russian troops will come</u>, for a time, fighting will erupt. Some states will stand together against the invasion. The economy of the nation will be greatly reduced. Food shortages will be normal. Hunger will be great. Disease will become of plague type proportions in some areas. Angelic leaders will openly reveal their presence and work. The Nation will have a rebirth and the greatest great awakening will occur. The Nation's capital will be relocated to a different region..."

* * * * * * * * *

It is interesting to note that the George Soros-funded *Black Lives Matter* movement caused racial tensions to build in the USA in 2016, in what a leaked memo revealed to be a plan to *"create a summer of chaos"* across America.

CHAPTER 13

Dumitru Duduman's Vision of Nuclear War in America (1984)

After being arrested, imprisoned and tortured for smuggling Bibles into Romania under Communist rule, Romanian preacher Dumitru Duduman was finally expelled from the country in 1984. After a failed attempt on his life, he escaped to America with his family. While preaching across Churches in America, he would share the following story...

* * * * * * * * *

"Late one night, I could not sleep. The children were sleeping on the luggage. My wife and daughter were crying, I went outside and walked around. I didn't want them to see me cry. I walked around the building, crying and saying, "God! Why did you punish me? Why did you bring me into this country? I can't understand anybody. If I try to ask anybody anything, all I hear is, "I don't know."

I stopped in front of the apartment and sat on a large rock. Suddenly a bright light came toward me. I jumped to my feet because it looked as if a car was coming directly at me, attempting to run me down! I thought the Romanian Secret Police had tracked me to America, and now they were trying to kill me. But it wasn't a car at all. As the light approached, it surrounded me. From the light I heard the same voice that I had heard so many times in prison.

He said "Dumitru, why are you so despaired?" I said, "Why did you punish me? Why did you bring me to this country? I have nowhere to lay my head down. I can't understand anybody." He said, "Dumitru, didn't I tell you I am here with you, also? I brought you to this country because this country will burn." I said, 'then why did you bring me here to burn? Why didn't you let me die in my own country? You should have let me die in jail in Romania! He said, "Dumitru, have patience so I can tell you. Get on this." I got on something next to him. I don't know what it was. I also know that I was not asleep. It was not a dream. It was not a vision. I was awake just as I am now.

He showed me all of California and said, "<u>This is Sodom and Gomorrah! All of this, in one day it will burn! Its sin has reached the Holy One</u>." Then he took me to Las Vegas. "This is Sodom and Gomorrah. In one day it will burn." Then he showed me the state of New York. "Do you know what this is?" he asked. I said, "No." He said "This is New York. This is Sodom and Gomorrah! In one day it will burn." Then he showed me all of Florida, "This is Florida." he said. "This is Sodom and Gomorrah! In one day it will burn."

Then he took me back home to the rock where we had begun. "IN ONE DAY IT WILL BURN! All of this I have shown you" – I said, "How will it burn?" He said, "Remember what I am telling you, because you will go on television, on the radio and in churches. You must yell with a loud voice. Do not be afraid, because I will be with you." I said, "How will I be able to go? Who knows me here in America? I don't know anybody here." He said, "Don't worry yourself. I will go before you. I will do a lot of healing in the American churches and I will open the doors for you. But do not say anything else besides what I tell you. This country will burn!"

I said, "What will you do with the church?" He said, "I want to save the church, but the churches have forsaken me." I said, "How did they forsake you?" He said, "The people praise themselves. The honor that the people are supposed to give Jesus Christ, they take upon themselves. In the churches there are divorces. There is adultery in the churches. There is abortion in the churches and all other sins that are possible.

Because of all the sin, I have left some of the churches. You must yell in a loud voice that they must put an end to their sinning. They must turn toward the Lord. The Lord never gets tired of forgiving. They must draw close to the Lord, and live a clean life. If they have sinned until now, they must put an end to it, and start a new life as the Bible tells them to live."

I said, "How will America burn?" America is the most powerful country in this world. Why did you bring us here to burn? Why didn't you at least let us die where all the Dudumans have died?"

He said, "Remember this, Dumitru. <u>The Russian spies have discovered where the nuclear warehouses are in America</u>. When the Americans will think that there is peace and safety – from the middle of the country, some of the people will start fighting against the government. The government will be busy with internal problems. Then from the ocean, from Cuba, Nicaragua, Mexico..." (He told me two other countries, but I didn't remember what they were.) "...they will bomb the nuclear warehouses. When they explode, America will burn!"

[...] <u>When America burns, the Lord will raise China, Japan, and other nations to go against the Russians.</u> They will beat the Russians and push them all the way to the gates of Paris.

Over there they will make a treaty, and appoint the Russians as their leaders. They will then unite against Israel. …When Israel realizes she does not have the strength of America behind her, she will be frightened. That's when she will turn to the Messiah for deliverance. That's when the Messiah will come. Then, the church will meet Jesus in the air, and he will bring them back with Him to the Mount of Olives (Jerusalem). At that time, the battle of Armageddon will be fought."

* * * * * * * * * *

Once again there is a theme of Russia invading the US, and Russian and Chinese troops marching through Europe (reaching "the gates of Paris"). But why would China and Japan appoint the Russians as their leaders, if they have defeated them? In any case, once more, the future looks bleak for the United States of America.

CHAPTER 14

Polish Priest Czeslaw Klimuszko's Vision of a Cataclysmic Destruction of Europe

In the 1980s, the Polish priest Czeslaw Klimuszko prophesied an invasion of Europe by a Muslim army, as well as a cataclysmic flooding of Europe. He stated:

> *"I saw soldiers crossing by sea on small, circular, sort of ships. By their faces it was obvious that they are not Europeans. I saw houses collapsing and Italian children who were crying. It was like an attack, the infidels in Europe. It seems I found that a great tragedy will meet Italy. The Italian shoe is submerged in water. Volcano or an earthquake? I saw the scene as a great cataclysm. It was horrible."*

He went on to say:

> *"War breaks out in the South... Russia will reveal its true colours... Fiery spears will strike the traitors. Will burn the whole town. Then the rockets will speed over the ocean, they will cross with others, will fall in sea water, will awaken the beast. She levers from the bottom, propelling a huge wave. I saw liners worn as husks... This mountain of water glides towards Europe. A new flood! Choke in Gibraltar! Pour inside Spain! Pour into the Sahara!*

Sinks the Italian Boot up the river Po. Rome shall disappear under water, with all the museums, with all the wonderful architecture... The sea will cover the archives. Documents bearing the seal of secrecy will now be lost forever. I saw up close this wall of water reaching Paris... higher than the Eiffel Tower... flowing inland it clutches people... Water glides with terrible power... they felt the power of the elements, which will sweep away everything... The scale of the disaster is breath-taking. And I saw it as if from the balcony, the whole area of the horizon. The water went by way of Germany, reaching Poland. Here, where we are today, we will be by the sea. Water will cover my graveyard. Millions in Poland will be doomed. But France and Germany will lose more. Italy will suffer the most. It will really unite Europe. Poverty is coming..."

* * * * * * * * *

Could a weapon of war cause a tsunami? Could a strike on the mid-Atlantic tectonic plate cause the flooding of both the Eastern seaboard and the European coastline? The recent Hollywood movie *The 5th Wave* alludes to such a scenario.

CHAPTER 15

Remote Viewer Ed Dames: The "Killshot"

Major Ed Dames is a Military Graduate of the University of California, a decorated military intelligence officer, and an original member of the U.S. Army prototype remote viewing training program. He retired from the army in 1991. He had served as the operations officer for the U.S. government's top secret psychic espionage unit.

In 1982, Ingo Swann developed a working model for how the unconscious mind communicates information to conscious awareness. To test the model, the Army sent Major Dames and five others to Swann as a prototype trainee group. The results exceeded all expectations.

Since the 1990s, Ed Dames has been sharing publicly some of the events he and his team "saw" when they remote-viewed our planet's future. Some of his predictions include:

❑ A global economic collapse, and the total economic collapse of the USA.

❑ China and Russia will become the new world leading super powers because they will have accumulated "all the gold in the world" (note: Russia and China are indeed currently stockpiling massive quantities of Gold)

- ❏ Many countries will defect from the petrodollar system and the western global recession will be much bigger than it is now. The US may be facing total collapse and the UK would back away from supporting the US. **A new currency will be introduced** because Russia and China are the largest producers and purchasers of gold.

- ❏ A coming 'Bird Flu epidemic' (virus) will further damage the economy.

- ❏ Because the US will lose their position and status in the world, China will make a power move against the US, backed by North Korea and Russia. The North Koreans are going to use a nuclear weapon, further taxing US military forces.

- ❏ <u>Israel will attack Iran, in what Dames called "an Armageddon-like situation</u>".

- ❏ A nuclear reactor will break down in Japan and leak out massive amounts of radiation *[the Fukushima disaster indeed occurred in 2011!]*

- ❏ Alien Contact will take place after 2014. Extra-terrestrial races have been observing humankind. A race similar to humans in appearance will "help us rebuild after the coming disasters".

- ❏ A mutation of a fungi – the damage will start in Africa and then it will be carried all the way across the Atlantic, by the winds and land in South America, and then to North America and do very big damage. It is a danger to grass, wheat, corn, and rye. This crop fungus was foreseen by remote viewers years in advance. It will devastate food supplies. *[Note: the killer fungus 'UG99' ("wheat rust") started in Africa and is currently spreading throughout the world…]*

- ❏ The Solar "Killshot" will occur, with the sun emitting some very large solar flares. The first series of flares will take down all electrical infrastructure. Don't be near the coast, he warns, as there will be many "Chernobyl-type" events, because the nuclear plants will break in half. People in some parts of the world may need to live underground, and have fresh sources of water to survive. Dames predicts it will be the largest global catastrophe ever seen in the history of mankind.

- ❏ Just before the 'Killshot' a nuclear explosion will occur in the Korean Peninsula, against the South Koreans and Americans, with a large number of casualties. This will be the last 'big' event before a large celestial object comes close to earth's orbit and creates large-scale disruption to our planet.

- ❏ A very large celestial body, planet-sized, will intersect Earth's orbit. There will be a sudden shift of Earth's axis of rotation. When that occurs, tsunamis, earthquakes, and eruptions of volcanoes will take place.

- ❏ An event will happen… where all warring soldiers look up to the sky… then *"drop their weapons to the ground and go home"*.

* * * * * * * * *

Below is a map created by Ed Dames, outlining some of the 'safe zones' on our planet, as well as new landmasses in the Atlantic and Pacific oceans, after these catastrophic 'Earth changes':

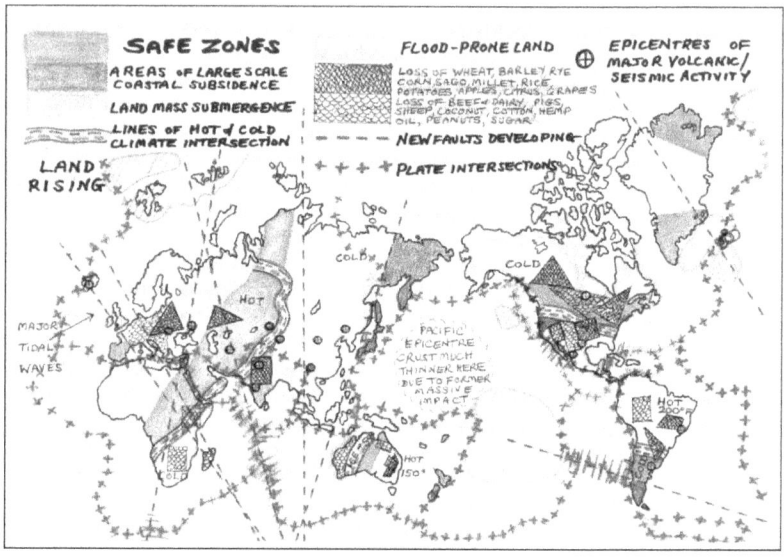

A map of Safe Zones following the solar "Killshot"

A psychic woman named Lynn Focus posted this comment online: *"As I look at one of his maps and tune into it, I get an overwhelming feeling of accuracy as he has outlined it. The one thing that really comes to me though is the timeframe in which he is referring to. I don't see this as one major event, but rather several events spanning over hundreds of years."*

CHAPTER 16

Joe Brandt's Vision of California Sinking Into The Pacific Ocean (1937)

The following vision was seen by Joe Brandt, age 17, while recovering from a brain concussion in a Fresno, California hospital in 1937, and echoes the visions of Michael Griffiths and Edgar Cayce.

* * * * * * * * *

"I woke up in the hospital room with a terrific headache--as if the whole world was revolving inside my brain. I remember, vaguely, the fall from my horse--Blackie. As I lay there, pictures began to form in my mind--pictures that stood still. I seemed to be in another world. Whether it was the future, or it was some ancient land, I could not say. Then slowly, like the silver screen of the "talkies", but with color and smell and sound, I seemed to find myself in Los Angeles--but I swear it was much bigger, and odd-shaped cars crowded the city streets.

I thought about Hollywood Boulevard, and I found myself there. Whether this is true, I do not know, but there were a lot of guys my age with beards and wearing, some of them, earrings. All the girls, some of them keen-o, wore real short skirts... and they slouched along-

-moving like a dance. Yet they seemed familiar. I wondered if I could talk to them, and I said, "Hello," but they didn't see or hear me. I decided I would look as funny to them as they looked to me.

I noticed there was a quietness about the air, a kind of stillness. Something else was missing, something that should be there. At first, I couldn't figure it out, I didn't know what it was--then I did. There were no birds. I listened. I walked two blocks north of the Boulevard-- all houses--no birds. I wondered what had happened to them. Had they gone away? Again, I could hear the stillness. Then I knew something was going to happen.

I wondered what year it was. It certainly was not 1937. I saw a newspaper on the corner with a picture of the President. It surely wasn't Mr. Roosevelt. He was bigger, heavier, big ears. If it wasn't 1937, I wondered what year it was... My eyes weren't working right. Someone was coming--someone in 1937--it was that darned, fat nurse ready to take my temperature. I woke up. Crazy dream.

[The next day]. Gosh, my headache is worse. It is a wonder I didn't get killed on that horse. I've had another crazy dream, back in Hollywood. Those people. Why do they dress like that, I wonder? Funny glow about them. It is a shine around their heads--something shining. I remember it now. I found myself back on the Boulevard. I was waiting for something to happen and I was going to be there. I looked up at the clock down by that big theater. It was ten minutes to four. Something big was going to happen.

I wondered if I went into a movie (since nobody could see me) if I'd like it. Some cardboard blond was draped over the marquee with her leg six feet long. I started to go in, but it wasn't inside. I was waiting for something to happen outside. I walked down the street. In the concrete they have names of stars. I just recognized a few of them. The other names I had never heard. I was getting bored, I wanted to get back to the hospital in Fresno, and I wanted to stay there on the Boulevard, even if nobody could see me. Those crazy kids. Why are

Chapter 16: Joe Brandt's Vision of California Sinking Into The Pacific Ocean (1937)

they dressed like that? Maybe it is some big Halloween doings, but it don't seem like Halloween. More like early spring. There was that sound again, that lack of sound. Stillness, stillness, stillness. The quiet is getting bigger and bigger. I know it is going to happen. Something is going to happen. It is happening now! It sure did. She woke me up, grinning and smiling, that fat one again.

"It's time for your milk, kiddo," she says. Gosh, old women of thirty acting like the cat's pajamas. Next time maybe she'll bring hot chocolate.

Where have I been? Where haven't I been? I've been to the ends of the earth and back. I've been to the end of the world--there isn't anything left. Not even Fresno, even though I'm lying here right this minute. If only my eyes would get a little clearer so I can write all this down. Nobody will believe me, anyway. I'm going back to that last moment on the Boulevard. Some sweet kid went past, dragging little boys (twins, I guess) by each hand. Her skirt was up--well, pretty high-- and she had a tired look. I thought for a minute I could ask her about the birds, what had happened to them, and then I remembered she hadn't seen me. Her hair was all frowzy, way out all over her head. A lot of them looked like that, but she looked so tired and like she was sorry about something. I guess she was sorry before it happened--because it surely did happen. There was a funny smell. I don't know where it came from. I didn't like it. A smell like sulphur, sulfuric acid, a smell like death. For a minute I thought I was back in chem [chemistry].

When I looked around for the girl, she was gone. I wanted to find her for some reason. It was as if I knew something was going to happen and I could stay with her, help her. She was gone, and I walked half a block, then I saw the clock again. My eyes seemed glued to that clock. I couldn't move. I just waited. It was five minutes to four on a sunny afternoon. I thought I would stand there looking at that clock forever waiting for something to come. Then, when it came, it was nothing. It was just nothing. It wasn't nearly as hard as the earthquake we had two years ago. The ground shook, just an instant. People looked at each other, surprised. Then they laughed. I laughed, too. So this was what I had been waiting for. This funny little shake. It meant nothing.

I was relieved and I was disappointed. What had I been waiting for? I started back up the Boulevard, moving my legs like those kids. How do they do it? I never found out. I felt as if the ground wasn't solid under me. I knew I was dreaming, and yet I wasn't dreaming. There was that smell again, coming up from the ocean. I was getting to the 5 and 10 store and I saw the look on the kids' faces. Two of them were right in front of me, coming my way.

"Let's get out of this place. Let's go back East." He seemed scared. It wasn't as if the sidewalks were trembling--but you couldn't seem to see them. Not with your eyes you couldn't. An old lady had a dog, a little white dog, and she stopped and looked scared, and grabbed him in her arms and said: "Let's go home, Frou, Frou. Mama is going to take you home." That poor lady, hanging on to her dog.

I got scared. Real scared. I remembered the girl. She was way down the block, probably. I ran and ran, and the ground kept trembling. I couldn't see it. I couldn't see it. But I knew it was trembling. Everybody looked scared. They looked terrible. One young lady just sat down on the sidewalk all doubled up. She kept saying, "earthquake, it's the earthquake," over and over. But I couldn't see that anything was different.
Then, when it came, how it came. Like nothing in God's world. Like nothing. It was like the scream of a siren, long and low, or the scream of a woman I heard having a baby when I was a kid. It was awful. It was as if something--some monster--was pushing up the sidewalks. You felt it long before you saw it, as if the sidewalks wouldn't hold you anymore. I looked out at the cars. They were honking, but not scared. They just kept moving. They didn't seem to know yet that anything was happening. Then, that white car, that baby half-sized

one came sprawling from the inside lane right against the curb. The girl who was driving just sat there. She sat there with her eyes staring, as if she couldn't move, but I could hear her. She made funny noises.

I watched her, thinking of the other girl. I said that it was a dream and I would wakeup. But I didn't wake up. The shaking had started again, but this time different. It was a nice shaking, like a cradle being rocked for a minute, and then I saw the middle of the Boulevard seem to be breaking in two. The concrete looked as if it were being pushed straight up by some giant shovel. It was breaking in two. That is why the girl's car went out of control. And then a loud sound again, like I've never heard before--then hundreds of sounds--all kinds of sounds; children, and women, and those crazy guys with earrings. They were all moving, some of them above the sidewalk. I can't describe it. They were lifted up... And the waters kept oozing--oozing. The cries. God, it was awful. I woke up. I never want to have that dream again.

It came again. Like the first time which was a preview and all I could remember was that it was the end of the world. I was right back there--all that crying. Right in the middle of it. My eardrums felt as if they were going to burst. Noise everywhere. People falling down, some of them hurt badly. Pieces of buildings, chips, flying in the air. One hit me hard on the side of the face, but I didn't seem to feel it. I wanted to wake up, to get away from this place. It had been fun in the beginning, the first dream, when I kind of knew I was going to dream the end of the world or something. This was terrible. There were older people in cars. Most of the kids were on the street. But those old guys were yelling bloody murder, as if anybody could help them. Nobody could help anybody. It was then I felt myself lifted up. Maybe I had died. I don't know. But I was over the city. It was tilting toward the ocean - like a picnic table.

The buildings were holding, better than you could believe. They were holding. They were holding. They were holding.

The people saw they were holding and they tried to cling to them or get inside. It was fantastic. Like a building had a will of its own. Everything else breaking around them, and they were holding, holding. I was up over them--looking down. I started to root for them. "Hold that line," I said. "Hold that line. Hold that line. Hold that line." I wanted to cheer, to shout, to scream. If the buildings held, those buildings on the Boulevard, maybe the girl--the girl with the two kids--maybe she could get inside. It looked that way for a long time, maybe three minutes, and three minutes was like forever. You knew they were going to hold, even if the waters kept coming up. Only they didn't.

I've never imagined what it would be like for a building to die. A building dies just like a person. It gives way, some of the bigger ones did just that. They began to crumble, like an old man with palsy, who couldn't take it anymore. They crumbled right down to nothing. And the little ones screamed like mad - over and above the roar of the people. They were mad about dying. But buildings die.

I couldn't look anymore at the people. I kept wanting to get higher. Then I seemed to be out of it all, but I could see. I seemed to be up on Big Bear near San Bernardino, but the funny thing was that I could see everywhere. I knew what was happening.

The earth seemed to start to tremble again. I could feel it even though I was high up. This time it lasted maybe twelve seconds, and it was gentle. You couldn't believe anything so gentle could cause so much damage. But then I saw the streets of Los Angeles--and everything between the San Bernardino mountains and Los Angeles. It was still tilting towards the ocean, houses, everything that was left. I could see the big lanes--dozens of big lanes still loaded with cars sliding the same way. Now the ocean was coming in, moving like a huge snake across the land. I wondered how long it was, and I could see the clock, even though I wasn't there on the Boulevard. It was 4:29. It had been half an hour. I was glad I couldn't hear the crying anymore. But I could see everything. I could see everything.

Then, like looking at a huge map of the world, I could see what was happening on the land and with the people. San Francisco was feeling it, but she was not in any way like Hollywood or Los Angeles. It was moving just like that earthquake movie with Jeanette McDonald and Gable. I could see all those mountains coming together... I knew it was going to happen to San Francisco--it was going to turn over--it would turn upside down. It went quickly, because of the twisting, I guess. It seemed much faster than Hollywood, but then I wasn't exactly there. I was a long way off. I was a long, long way off. I shut my eyes for a long time--I guess ten minutes--and when I opened them I saw Grand Canyon.

<u>*When I looked at Grand Canyon, that great big gap was closing in, and Boulder Dam was being pushed, from underneath*</u>*. And then, Nevada, and on up to Reno. Way down south, way down. Baja, California. Mexico too. It looked like some volcano down there was erupting, along with everything else. I saw the map of South America, especially Columbia. Another volcano--eruption--shaking violently. I seemed to be seeing a movie of three months before--before the Hollywood earthquake.* <u>*Venezuela seemed to be having some kind of volcanic activity*</u>*. Away off in the distance, I could see Japan, on a fault, too. It was so far off--not easy to see because I was still on Big Bear Mountain, but it started to go into the sea. I couldn't hear screaming, but I could see the surprised look on their faces. They looked so surprised. Japanese girls are made well, supple, easy, muscles that move well. Pretty, too. But they were all like dolls. It was so far away I could hardly see it. In a minute or two it seemed over. Everybody was gone. There was nobody left.*

I didn't know time now. I couldn't see a clock. I tried to see the island of Hawaii. I could see huge tidal waves beating against it. The people on the streets were getting wet, and they were scared. But I didn't see anybody go into the sea.

I seemed way around the globe. More flooding. Is the world going to be drenched? <u>Constantinople. Black Sea rising.</u> Suez Canal, for some reason seemed to be drying up. <u>Sicily--she doesn't hold.</u> I could see a map. Mt Etna. Mt. Etna is shaking. A lot of area seemed to go, but it seemed to be earlier or later. I wasn't sure of time, now.

<u>England--huge floods--but no tidal waves</u>. Water, water everywhere, but no one was going into the sea. People were frightened and crying. Some places they fell to the streets on their knees and started to pray for the world. I didn't know the English were emotional. Ireland, Scotland--all kinds of churches were crowded--it seemed night and day. People were carrying candles <u>and everybody was crying for California, Nevada, parts of Colorado</u>--maybe even all of it, even Utah. Everybody was crying--most of them didn't even know anybody in California, Nevada, Utah, but they were crying as if they were blood kin. Like one family. Like it happened to them.

<u>New York was coming into view--she was still there, nothing had happened, yet the water level was way up</u>. Here, things were different. People were running in the streets yelling--"end of the world." Kids ran into restaurants and ate everything in sight. I saw a shoe store with all the shoes gone in about five minutes. 5th Avenue--everybody running. Some radio blasting--bigger--a loud speaker--that in a few minutes, power might be shut off. They must control themselves. Five girls were running like mad toward the Y.M.C.A., that place on Lexington or somewhere. But nothing was happening in New York. I saw an old lady with garbage cans filling them with water. Everybody seemed scared to death. Some people looked dazed. The streets seemed filled with loud speakers. It wasn't daylight. It was night.

I saw, like the next day, and everything was topsy turvey. Loud speakers again about fuel tanks broken in areas--shortage of oil. People seemed to be looting markets.

Chapter 16: Joe Brandt's Vision of California Sinking Into The Pacific Ocean (1937)

I saw a lot of places that seemed safe, and people were not so scared. Especially the rural areas. Here everything was almost as if nothing had happened. People seemed headed to these places, some on foot, some in cars that still had fuel. I heard--or somehow I knew--that <u>somewhere in the Atlantic land had come up</u>. A lot of land. I was getting awfully tired. I wanted to wake up. I wanted to go back to the girl--to know where she was--and those two kids. I found myself back in Hollywood--and it was still 4:29. I wasn't up on Big Bear at all, I was perched over Hollywood. I was just there. It seemed perfectly natural in my dream.

I could hear now. I could hear, someplace, a radio station blasting out--telling people not to panic. They were dying in the streets. There were picture stations with movies--some right in Hollywood--these were carrying on with all the shaking. One fellow in the picture station was a little short guy who should have been scared to death. But he wasn't. He kept shouting and reading instructions. Something about helicopters or planes would go over--some kind of planes--but I knew they couldn't. Things were happening in the atmosphere. The waves were rushing up now. Waves. Such waves. Nightmare waves.

Then, I saw again. Boulder Dam, going down--pushing together, pushing together breaking apart--no, Grand Canyon was pushing together, and <u>Boulder Dam was breaking apart</u>. It was still daylight. All these radio stations went off at the same time--Boulder Dam had broken.

I wondered how everybody would know about it--people back East. That was when I saw the "ham radio operators." I saw them in the darndest places, as if I were right there with them. Like the little guy with glasses, they kept sounding the alarm. One kept saying: "<u>This is California. We are going into the sea</u>. This is California. We are going into the sea. Get to high places. Get to the mountains. All states west--this is California. We are going into the...we are going into the..." I thought he was going to say "sea," but I could see him. He was inland, but the waters had come in. His hand was still *clinging to the table, he was trying to get up, so that once again he could say: "This is California. We are going into the sea. This is California. We are going into the sea."*

I seemed to hear this, over and over, for what seemed hours--just those words--they kept it up until the last minute--all of them calling out, "Get to the mountains--this is California. We are going into the sea."

I woke up. It didn't seem as if I had been dreaming. I have never been so tired. For a minute or two, I thought it had happened. I wondered about two things. I hadn't seen what happened to Fresno and I hadn't found out what happened to that girl.

I've been thinking about it all morning. I'm going home tomorrow. It was just a dream. It was nothing more. Nobody in the future on Hollywood Boulevard is going to be wearing earrings--and those beards. Nothing like that is ever going to happen. That girl was so real to me--that girl with those kids. It won't ever happen--but if it did, how could I tell her (maybe she isn't even born yet) to move away from California when she has her twins--and she can't be on the Boulevard that day. She was so gosh-darned real.

The other thing--those ham operators--hanging on like that--over and over--saying the same thing: "This is California. We are going into the sea. This is California. We are going into the sea. Get to the mountains. Get to the hilltops. California, Nevada, Colorado, Arizona, Utah. This is California. We are going into the sea."

I guess I'll hear that for days." (Source: *"California Superquake"* written by Paul James)

* * * * * * * * *

Is this super-quake going to happen soon? Do people need to move out of California right now? Probably not, but if you *do*

Chapter 16: Joe Brandt's Vision of California Sinking Into The Pacific Ocean (1937)

live in that region, be on the lookout for major volcanic activity and earthquakes along this fault line...

I love California – San Diego, San Francisco, and Vancouver in Canada are a few of my favourite cities in the world – but I wouldn't move there just now, all the same.

CHAPTER 17

Greek Orthodox Elder Joseph of Vatopedino Warns of World War III

The Greek Orthodox priest, Elder Joseph, of the Vatopedino Monastery of Agion Oros, made some startling prophetic predictions in the 1970s. I grew up in Greece, so I speak the language. Here follows my translation of one of his recorded speeches.

* * * * * * * * *

"There will be a major political upheaval. When this happens, the international capital will be withdrawn. The Jewish capital. When this international capital gets withdrawn, all the employees will become unemployed. Greece will become impoverished and the people will starve. That is when the Turkish provocation (assault) will occur, during all this upheaval…

Russia will respond by invading Turkey. The Russians will be victorious, but they will want to keep Constantinople and the Straights for themselves. Russia will only hold on for two or three months. The Jewish world, together with the Americans, will take action, and amass around the Byzantium. Because Byzantium was uprooted by the Vatican, and handed over to the Turks... So their descendants will be collected by the Justice of the Lord, on the borders of Byzantium...

Over a period of three days of slaughter, there will be more than 700 million dead. Not a single man will come home... Not women and children... men. The entire City will be destroyed. Only the church of Aghia Sophia shall remain. And that is when the reconstruction will begin. We will return to our roots.

Greece will become impoverished... dramatically... but it will return. It won't stay in that state. We will return to our roots. The Pontus, Asia Minor, and [...] all of that is ours. It is the lands of our ancestors.

When the Americans and the Jews will push back, that is when an angel will appear in the Heavens, and will cause them much drunkenness. They will lose their senses. Not to make them crazy... but to inspire rabid hatred within them, where they will desire to kill one another.

The Americans will bring many mercenaries, too. Japanese mercenaries, and others. For the aim of the Jews is for Christianity to be uprooted from the Earth.

700 million will perish in three days. Then the angel in the Heavens will appear again, and order them to stop. They will awaken, and ask themselves "Why did we murder each other?" They will awaken and return to their Europe, the few who remain. The angel will then resurrect those who sleep since the time of Byzantium, the political and ecclesiastic leaders of that time, and will point them out with his finger and say: "Take these men and have them rule over you." That is when the re-formation of the human race will begin.

The Gods shall dwell with the humans. There will be so much wealth, so much peace, so much happiness, for three or four decades, so that the Christians may get organised... with the Antichrist amongst them... And then... Concordance ('synteleia'), the End of the Age will occur." When asked about whether these events would take place 'in our time', he replied that they would probably occur during "the generation of our children". When probed further about when exactly this would all take place, he replied:

"God never shows us the exact time, but the signs around us are harbingers. There will be political upheaval. The international capital will be withdrawn, and then all the employees will be fired."

Elder Joseph mentions that *"the Vatican handed Byzantium to the Turks"* and the *"Jews want to uproot Christianity"*. It would appear that age-old rifts between the Orthodox Church, the Catholic Church (the Vatican), and the Jewish faith, going back thousands of years, are still very present on the minds of the respective religious leaders. Could this way of thinking lead to armed conflict?

"The Turks will know three days earlier than the Christians when the war will begin... After the dissolution of Turkey, the Russians will continue the war till the Persian Gulf and stop their troops outside of Jerusalem. Then the western powers will give a deadline to withdraw their army and start gathering to attack Russia."

Saint Paisios of Mount Athos 1924 – 1994

"A time will come when the Russian race will go down to the Middle East and Jerusalem... First Austria (Yugoslavia) will be dissolved, then Turkey."

Saint Kosmas of Aetolia 1714 – 1779

Prophecy 2017 – 2137

* * * * * * * * *

Here follows Elder Joseph's prophecy, translated from George Boura's 1972 book, *Spiritual Covenant*:

"Listen people of the world, and you, reader, pay close attention to what you are about to read… They may be hard to swallow, and sorrowful, but these events are destined to be… These words were written by our fathers for the world to know the terrible consequences of the coming war. So that you may turn to God and repent, to save yourself and live a joyful life.

A seemingly insignificant event will suddenly spark the fires of war; a war cry is coming from Bulgaria… Suddenly shall Russia invade Turkey, and like a gushing stream conquer all of Persia. She shall march without great resistance headlong into Palestine… The Antichrist wants to become the God of our world… Then shall the Western nations intervene… Woe to the states of the North, which are all turned to dust.

With great rage does the Bear (Russia) defend itself valiantly in Turkey, which did great injustice to Greece, and is burning like a candle. In vain does the Bear try to hold on to the Straights, and in the end shall she stand no more. That is because from the East, from Korea and Manchuria, do Japan and America invade, and march full speed towards Siberia, while in the western front shall Germany be victorious. It shall be impossible for Russia to hold and she will abandon the Straights, Turkey and Egypt. The Bear is hit from every direction and leaves in a great rush like the undisciplined cattle. Then, however, shall the treacherous Turkey also be defeated, for she will commit great treason. Because, after she is conquered whole by Russia, she will ally with Bulgaria.

All Christians that live in the City (Constantinople) and in the neighbouring lands must leave. For the City will burn and no one will remain alive in her. Only the temple of Aghia Sofia will remain standing, the temple of God's wisdom which will illuminate the entire holy kingdom of Christ, whom the world eagerly awaits.

The first phase of this terrible war is over; is all this terrible suffering not enough, Oh Lord? A new war will break out and woe to Man for what he has to suffer. The issue of the City (Jerusalem? Constantinople?) will once more be at the crux, and the world will be entangled in such a way that it will not untangle.

Immediately does discord ensue in Crete, where the passions and hatreds light up. Since the powerful of the earth will be let down, war occurs, the likes of which the world has never seen. Woe to the wicked ones, for none shall remain.

Then shall Greece, neutral, and always victimized, ask for the injustices to be righted. She will remain ready and awaiting, without interfering in the war. Then will she talk, when the Lord's voice from the heavens shall be heard; then shall she be vindicated.

The nations will be slaughtering each other with great ferocity in the vicinity of the City, to gain control of the Straights. Then will the calf be drowned in blood. Then shall the wheat be separated from the chaff. In the Sea no ship shall remain, and from the blood will the Sea become red. The City will burn whole, and not a trace of man shall remain, because much has she committed. Only the temple of Aghia Sofia shall remain.

Three days shall the battle last, and he who comes out alive may consider himself particularly fortunate. Eighteen nations with great ferocity will be slaughtering without sense, bathed in blood. On the third day, those exhausted from battle will be startled to see, up high in the Heavens, that a star brighter than the Sun will be. And from below the star, a Cross will shine in flames, burning red, and startled, will the Nations hear from the Heaven the thunderous voice of an Angel, suddenly, that will make them stand to attention.

Their weapons shall they drop to the ground, gazing, petrified from fear.

Remain still, for the Voice to be heard. Remain still, for enough has the blood of man been shed. Rush to the place towards the right, and follow the arrow coming forth from the Star. There shall you find the holy man of mine. Shepherd have I chosen him to be, for my flock. Him have you also elected a shepherd, so that he may guide my sheep, that have wandered alone all these years without a home. At night-time shall My Voice be heard, and the world, terrified and startled, shall see the arrow be directed South, towards Greece, that from the heavenly light shall shine like a torch.

Then shall ambassadors reach Greece, and with great delight shall Greece respond. Then shall Greece rise up with her army, so that she may fulfil her holy purpose: to reclaim without fight, the holy places which her enemies had conquered, as the world acknowledges. Then shall the refugees, with great delight, return back to their homes like flying eagles. Then shall the Greek King, the chosen of the Lord, which in everything shall be perfect, rule the Earth with great justice. And the Earth shall know lasting peace.

The weapons of war will be turned into tools and ploughs for farming, and peace and happiness will reign on the earth. People will live like brothers on the earth, and none will ask another whether he is a stranger, but will address each other as brothers descended from Adam.

The Greeks shall come back, this is the truth, do not be believe the unbelievers that it is false. All of this is destined to be, the time is nigh; The entire Universe will shake but you shall not be frightened. The coming calamity will smite the impious and wicked ones, and without remorse wipe them off the face of the earth.
Think logically and make the decision, if you want to live and be saved eternally, that you all repent and turn towards the Divine, for nowhere else is there salvation.

Chapter 17: Greek Orthodox Elder Joseph of Vatopedino Warns of World War III

A war is coming the likes of which the world has never seen, of such terrifying scale and horror, and no peace shall be had until the wheat is separated from the chaff and the pests have burned away like the dry grass."

* * * * * * * * *

"I cannot rule out that, in certain circumstances, local and regional armed conflicts could grow into a large-scale war, possibly even with nuclear weapons... Russia could be involved in a conflict where weapons of mass destruction could be used... The possibility of local armed conflicts virtually along the entire perimeter of the Russian border has grown dramatically."

General Makarov, Chief of the General Staff of the Armed Forces of Russia and First Deputy Minister of Defence, May 3rd 2012

* * * * * * * * *

It is interesting to note that remote viewer Ed Dames saw all the armies of the world "looking up" and then going home (see *Chapter 15*). What is this 'event in the sky' that will cause such a reaction? Will we see 'an angel'? Will this be a real event or a staged 'holographic projection'?

As for the "international capital" being withdrawn, that is a very real possibility. In today's era of globalization, international investment capital can flow into a country on a massive scale (e.g. huge capital investments flowing into China since 1990), but can also *flee* a country at an equally rapid pace (see Argentina, or the 1997 Asian crisis).

What if the investment class gets "spooked" by some major financial or geopolitical event (e.g. a stock market crash, or nuclear war) and withdraw their capital *suddenly and at the same time* from companies, the stock market, and even from the banking system? What if the banking system collapses? What if oil supplies were to suddenly stop? Any one of these events could lead to thousands of companies being unable to pay their employees, and <u>hundreds of millions of employees becoming *de facto* unemployed overnight.</u> That is why I have urged my clients for over a decade to become *resourceful,* start their own business, have multiple sources of income, and become less reliant on the current *system*. Now, this advice extends to storing Gold and Silver, becoming self-sufficient in water, food production, and even electric power.

When The Lights of New York Go Out For The Last Time

"Ayn Rand's book Atlas Shrugged is a step-by-step plan on how to take over America. Everything that is happening is conspired to happen. In the book, they gain control of the world by bankrupting their own businesses. The illuminati own most stores you step foot in, 99.9% of them, and they will destroy them on purpose. They are buying up all the stores and companies, and they plan to bankrupt them all, until... Their plan is to bankrupt the whole world, where nothing has any value, and the currency does not exist anywhere, and then come back and solve all the problems... She spent a third of the book describing how they would raise the oil prices and then later destroy the oil fields and then they would also completely shut down the coal... Atlas Shrugged ended with this: "When the lights of New York City go out for the last time, we will have the World!" ...If you live in a large city, how are you going to get your food if they don't bring it to you? Everything will be paralyzed, nothing will move... You must be dependent on the Federal Government for every bite of food, every light bulb in your house and every warmth that you feel coming through your homes."

John Todd, 1972

"The Secret Government is planning to create industrial depression and financial panic, unemployment, hunger, shortage of food, use this to control the masses and the mobs, and use the mobs to wipe out all those who dare stand in the way. All the experts I speak to are talking about 'food shortages'. It's coming."

Ted Gunderson, former FBI agent

CHAPTER 18

Prophetic Visions of Baba Vanga Pandeva, The "Nostradamus of the Balkans"

Baba Vanga Pandeva was born on January 31, 1911, on the territory of modern Macedonia. Having lived in Bulgaria for most of her life, she died on August 11, 1996. She was recognized as one of the great visionaries of the twentieth century, and was known in the region as "the Nostradamus of the Balkans". Millions of people around the world are convinced of her psychic abilities.

Vanga lost her sight at the age of 12, after being swept away by a tornado. She started making predictions when she was 16, but her abilities grew after she turned 30.

She foretold the break-up of the Soviet Union, the Chernobyl disaster, and the date of Stalin's death, among many other predictions. It is said that many statesmen visited Vanga, seeking out her insights into their futures, including Adolf Hitler. After the Second World War, Bulgarian politicians and leaders from different Soviet Republics, including Leonid Brezhnev, and Yeltsin, sought her counsel.

Several researchers and psychiatrists have studied her ability to see into the future, and reportedly, some of the studies concluded that **approximately 80% of her predictions turned out to be accurate**.

She would claim that "distance and time" do not matter, and that beings from the spirit world were communicating this information to her.

Her prophecies include the following:

- In 1989 she predicted the attacks on the Twin Towers: *"The American brethren will fall after being attacked by the steel birds. The wolves will be howling in a bush, and innocent blood will be gushing."*

- According to Baba Vanga, 2016 would be the year that *"Muslims will invade Europe".*

- Things will start to deteriorate for America and <u>the "African American" president will be the last acting president of the United States</u>...

- She prophesied that in 2018 China will be the dominant "super power" in the world, taking the lead from the already worn U.S.

- Also in 2018, a space probe will discover "a new form of energy" on planet Venus.

- <u>A *"Great Islamic war"* would begin in Syria, culminating in complete control of Rome, in 2043</u> (a Muslim invasion of Europe). She also prophesied that a new Caliphate would be established and that Europe *"would cease to exist"*, the continent becoming *"almost empty, wastelands devoid of any form of life."* The population of Europe will disappear as a result of wars.

❑ She predicted that Communism would return to Europe, and would spread to the rest of the world.

❑ She also stated that in 2023 the Earth's orbit would change, which would "melt the poles" and "set fire in the Middle East". Water levels will rise due to the melting of the poles. There will be a rebirth of nature.

❑ In 200 years, men will make contact with 'brothers in mind' from other worlds. She claimed that many aliens have been living on Earth for a very long time. Aliens will help man to live underwater in 2130. She also predicted that a war might take place on planet Mars in 3005.

❑ There will be an attempt to travel to other planets, with the hope of finding other sources of energy to Earth.

❑ A comet reaches the Moon, so the Earth is covered by a ring of rocks and ashes. Mars is threatened by a comet.

❑ Earth will experience a global drought.

❑ A new sun will illuminate the dark side of our planet. This could refer to a scientific project that began in 2008, that will create an artificial sun using nuclear energy *(see the predictions of Stewart Swerdlow, in Chapter 22).*

❑ The Earth will die, but mankind will have advanced enough to move to a new solar system.

Baba Vanga had a prophetic dream, in which she was told that she would die on August 11th, and be buried two days later. She added that a ten-year-old blind girl living in France was to inherit her gift, and that people would soon hear about her.

Baba Vanga died on the 11th of August, 1996.

> In early August 1976, just two months before her death, Bosnian actress and singer Silvana Armenulić was on tour in Bulgaria and decided to seize the opportunity to meet with Baba Vanga. The meeting was unpleasant. Vanga only sat and stared out a window with her back to Silvana. She did not speak.
>
> After a long time, Vanga finally spoke: "Nothing. You do not have to pay. I do not want to speak with you. Not now. Go and come back in three months." As Silvana turned around and walked towards the door, Vanga said: "Wait. In fact, you will not be able to come. Go, go. If you can come back in three months, do so."
>
> Silvana took this as confirmation that she would die and left Vanga's home in tears. Armenulić died two months later, 10 October 1976, in a car crash with her sister Mirjana. (Source: Wikipedia)

CHAPTER 19

Will There Be a 'One World Government'?

I have listed in the final few chapters of this book the predictions by people who claim to have worked for a secret international organization intent on forming a "One World Government". This organization has had to operate in the shadows, they claim, because no government or people would accept to relinquish their national sovereignty, even for the purpose of achieving "World peace" (if there are no nations, there can be no more wars *between* nations).

Taking the (really) long view, I am not opposed to having a "global" government on our planet. Assuming ours is not the only civilization in the Universe (highly unlikely), it is hard to imagine that advanced alien civilizations out there in the Cosmos would still have something as antiquated as "nations" on their planets – it would seem extremely old-fashioned and inefficient. But could such an outcome ever be achieved peacefully and democratically?

Is there a plan by the 'Elite' of this world to create a unified global government? The following statements would certainly point in that direction:

"We are grateful to the Washington Post, The New York Times, Time Magazine and other great publications whose directors have attended our meetings and respected their promises of discretion for almost forty years. It would have been impossible for us to develop our plan for the world if we had been subjected to the lights of publicity during those years. But, the world is now more sophisticated and prepared to march towards a world government. The supranational sovereignty of an intellectual elite and world bankers is surely preferable to the national auto-determination practiced in past centuries."
—David Rockefeller, Baden-Baden, Germany 1991

"The 'affirmative task' before us is to create a New World Order."
–VP Joe Biden, speech Import Export Bank, April 5, 2013

"Each of us has the hope to build a New World Order."
–President Richard Nixon, Hangzhou, China, February 1972

"I think that his [Obama's] task will be to develop an overall strategy for America in this period, when really a New World Order can be created."
—Henry Kissinger, CNBC 2008

"In the next century, nations as we know it will be obsolete; all states will recognize a single, global authority. National sovereignty wasn't such a great idea after all."
—Strobe Talbot, Deputy Secretary of State, TIME, July 1992

"We are on the verge of a global transformation. All we need is the right major crisis and the nations will accept the New World Order."
—David Rockefeller

Chapter 19: Will There Be a 'One World Government'?

"We have before us the opportunity to forge, for ourselves and for future generations, a New World Order. A world where the rule of law, not the law of the jungle, rules all nations. When we are successful–and we will be–we have a real chance at this New World Order. An order in which a credible United Nations can use its peacekeeping forces to fulfil the promise and vision of its founders."
—George H.W. Bush, March 21, 1991

"Today, America would be outraged if U.N. troops entered Los Angeles to restore order. Tomorrow they will be grateful! This is especially true if they were told that there were an outside threat from beyond, whether real or promulgated, that threatened our very existence. It is then that all peoples of the world will plead to deliver them from this evil. The one thing every man fears is the unknown. When presented with this scenario, individual rights will be willingly relinquished for the guarantee of their well-being granted to them by the World Government."
–Dr. Henry Kissinger, Evian, France, 1991

"We shall have World Government, whether or not we like it. The only question is whether World Government will be achieved by consent or conquest."
–James Paul Warburg, Wall Street banker, February 7, 1950

"The Final Act of the Uruguay Round, marking the conclusion of the most ambitious trade negotiation of our century, will give birth – in Morocco – to the World Trade Organization, the third pillar of the New World Order, along with the United Nations and the International Monetary Fund."
Government of Morocco, advertisement, New York Times, April 1994

"The real truth of the matter is, as you and I know, that a financial element in the larger centers has owned the Government ever since the days of Andrew Jackson."
—Franklin D. Roosevelt, letter to Col. House, November 21, 1933

"...all of us here at the policy-making level have had experience with directives... from the White House.... The substance of them is that we shall use our grant-making power so as to alter our life in the United States that we can be comfortably merged with the Soviet Union."
—H. Rowan Gaither, Jr., President – Ford Foundation (told to Norman Dodd, Congressional Reese Commission 1954)

"By the end of this decade we will live under the first One World Government that has ever existed in the society of nations... a government with absolute authority to decide the basic issues of survival. One world government is inevitable."
—Pope John Paul II

"All of us will ultimately be judged on the effort we have contributed to building a New World Order."
—Robert Kennedy, presidential candidate and US Attorney General, 1967

"Fundamental Bible-believing people do not have the right to indoctrinate their children in their religious beliefs because we, the state, are preparing them for the year 2000, when America will be part of a one-world global society and their children will not fit in."
–Nebraska State Sen. Peter Hoagland, radio interview, 1983.

"Some even believe we are a part of a secret cabal working against the best interests of the United States, characterizing my family and me as 'internationalists' and of conspiring with others around the world to build a more integrated global political and economic structure – one world, if you will. If that's the charge, I stand guilty and I am proud of it."
—David Rockefeller, *Memoirs*

"The interests behind the Bush administration, such as the CFR, the Trilateral Commission – founded by Brzezinski for David Rockefeller – and the Bilderberg Group have prepared for and are now moving to implement open world dictatorship within the next five years."
–Dr. Johannes Koeppl, Former German Ministry for Defence official, advisor to NATO

"To achieve world government, it is necessary to remove from the minds of men, their individualism, loyalty to family traditions, national patriotism and religious dogmas."
—G. Brock Chisholm, co-founder of the World Federation for Mental Health, former director of UN World Health Organization

"The governments of the present day have to deal not merely with other governments, with emperors, kings and ministers, but also with the secret societies which have everywhere their unscrupulous agents, and can at the last moment upset all the governments' plans. […] The world is governed by very different personages from what is imagined by those who are not behind the scenes."
—Benjamin Disraeli, Prime Minister of England 1874-1880, *Coningsby*

"The real rulers in Washington are invisible, and exercise power from behind the scenes."
—Felix Frankfurter, Supreme Court Justice, 1952

"Whatever happens, whatever the outcome, New World Order is going to come into the world… It will be buttressed with police power…When peace comes this time there is going to be a New World Order of social justice. It cannot be another Versailles."
—Edward VIII, King of England, 1936

"Three hundred men, all of-whom know one another, direct the economic destiny of Europe and choose their successors from among themselves."
—Walter Rathenau, Prime Minister of Germany until he was assassinated in 1922.

"It is the sacred principles enshrined in the United Nations charter to which the American people will henceforth pledge their allegiance."
–George HW Bush, 1992

Are these statements above true? Or are they merely 'wild conspiracy theories'? Will there be a single Global Government on our planet? Time will tell.

CHAPTER 20

Albert Pike's Vision of Three World Wars and 'a Formidable Social Cataclysm' (1871)

In a letter written by Albert Pike, a Freemason, in 1871, he describes the following vision he received of three world wars and a coming 'formidable social cataclysm'.

* * * * * * * * *

"The First World War must be brought about in order to overthrow the power of the Czars in Russia and make that country a fortress of atheistic Communism. The divergences caused by the "agentur" (agents) of the Illuminati between the British and Germanic Empires will be used to foment this war. At the end of the war, Communism will be built and used in order to destroy the other governments and in order to weaken the religions."

"The Second World War must be fomented by taking advantage of the differences between the Fascists and the political Zionists. This war must be brought about so that Nazism is destroyed and that the political Zionism be strong enough to institute a sovereign state of Israel in Palestine. During the Second World War, International Communism must become strong enough in order to balance Christendom, which would be then restrained and held in check

until the time when we would need it for the final social cataclysm."

"The Third World War must be fomented by taking advantage of the differences caused by the "agentur" of the Illuminati between the political Zionists and the leaders of the Islamic World. The war must be conducted in such a way that Islam (the Moslem Arabic World) and political Zionism (the State of Israel) mutually destroy each other. Meanwhile the other nations, once more divided on this issue will be constrained to fight to the point of complete physical, moral, spiritual and economical exhaustion...

We shall unleash the Nihilists and the atheists, and we shall provoke a formidable social cataclysm which in all its horror will show clearly to the nations the effect of absolute atheism, origin of savagery and of the most bloody turmoil.

Then everywhere, the citizens, obliged to defend themselves against the world minority of revolutionaries, will exterminate those destroyers of civilization, and the multitude, disillusioned with Christianity, whose deistic spirits will from that moment be without compass or direction, anxious for an ideal, but without knowing where to render its adoration, will receive the true light through the universal manifestation of the pure doctrine of Lucifer, brought finally out in the public view.

This manifestation will result from the general reactionary movement which will follow the destruction of Christianity and atheism, both conquered and exterminated at the same time."

* * * * * * * * *

This letter, dated August 15, 1871, was sent to Giuseppe Mazzini, a Thirty-Third Degree Mason, who was the founder of the Scottish Rite of Freemasonry in Italy. Interestingly, Mazzini would later express his desire to create a "United States of

Europe", a century before the European Union came into existence.

Mazzini is also the founder of the MAFIA. With the purported goal of freeing Italy from the control of the monarchy and the Pope, he founded a group of revolutionaries called 'Young Italy'. They funded themselves *"by robbing banks, looting or burning businesses if protection money was not paid, and kidnapping for ransom. Throughout Italy the word spread that "Mazzini autorizza furti, incendi e attentati," meaning, 'Mazzini authorizes theft, arson, and kidnapping.' This phrase was shortened to the acronym, M.A.F.I.A. Organized crime was born."* (source: John Daniel, "Scarlet and the Beast")

* * * * * * * * *

Reassuringly, this letter was shown to be a 'hoax', in the early 1900s. At least that's what the authorities and the press told the people, at the time.

Still, it is interesting to note that the political alliances between England and Germany, forged between 1871 and 1898 by Prussian politician and Freemason Otto von Bismarck, were instrumental in bringing about the First World War…

In 1945, at the Potsdam Conference eight weeks after the unconditional surrender of Germany, a large portion of Europe was simply handed over to Russia. And on November 29, 1947, the United Nations General Assembly voted in favour of a Partition Plan that created the State of Israel in Palestine.

Now we are seeing Europe and the Middle East being destabilized by "The Arab Spring", "War in Syria", "ISIS", and "waves of refugees".

Could the Global Financial Collapse, the collapse of America, instability and wars in the Middle East, as well as waves of refugees, be part of a planetary agenda for global change? Could all this upheaval be facilitating a period of 'purification' that our planet needs, before a 'Golden Age' of '*1000 years of peace and enlightenment*'? Or is this merely propaganda?

> "*Masonry, like all the Religions, all the Mysteries... conceals its secrets from all except the Adepts and Sages, or the Elect, and uses false explanations and misinterpretations of its symbols to mislead those who deserve only to be misled; to conceal the Truth, which it calls Light, from them, and to draw them away from it. Truth is not for those who are unworthy or unable to receive it, or would pervert it.... Every age has had a religion suited to its capacity... The truth must be kept secret, and the masses need a teaching proportioned to their imperfect reason...*"
>
> Albert Pike, *Morals and Dogma*

CHAPTER 21

Stewart Swerdlow's Predictions (2002)

Stewart Swerdlow worked in an underground military facility at Montauk Point for more than a decade. As a psychic and former 'insider', he made the following predictions in his book *"True Blood, Blue Blood"*, published in 2002, about what would happen in America over the coming decades. These events would be orchestrated by the ruling class, he explained, in order to facilitate the acceptance by the American public of the need for a *global government*:

- ❑ Americans have grown too "rich and self-righteous" to agree to being part of a *'One World Government'*. Since it would not make sense for Americans to unite with weaker countries, the agenda calls for the US to be deindustrialized, bankrupt, and reduced to the state of a "Third World Country". The US leadership works towards this long-term agenda.

- ❑ Fuel reserves in America will be eliminated. Severe weather patterns will be created with weather control technology, to force the population to consume the remaining fuel. Utilities will be unable to cope with the demand.

- Large regional natural disasters will be created with weather control technology, so that local civil authorities are unable to cope. [*As I write this, Louisiana is flooded in what is being described as a "1000-year flood".*]

- Rioting and chaos will be promoted in major US cities. Polarization of minorities will create a call from the minorities for a need for segregation. [*This appears to be happening right now in cities across America…*]

- There will be an economic/stock market collapse as a result of the disasters, lack of utilities, and planned chaos.

- The President will enact Executive Orders that in effect, will rescind the Constitution and civil rights. **Martial Law will be declared**, "to restore order". The United Nations will be called in to restore order. Chinese, Russian, and German troops are already stationed around the United States borders.

- Dissidents will be shipped for re-education to huge **concentration camps** already in place in the United States and Canada.

- The United Nations will declare that the US is too large to be administered as is, and will order it to be split into two districts: Eastern and Western. The Eastern district capital will be Atlanta. The Western district capital will be Denver. This is why government offices and international super-airports were built in these two cities.

- New York City will be declared the United Nations capital city for the Earth and given special status. This is why New York State is called the "Empire State."

Chapter 21: Stewart Swerdlow's Predictions (2002)

- ❑ Undesirables will be eliminated via chemtrails, mosquito spraying," flu shots, and other inoculations. Radicals will simply be executed.

- ❑ All air force bases will be staging areas [to process people, refugees, military personnel].

"Tomorrow we will stand master of the world, borne to victory on the wings of the Valkyrie. Our enemies' weapons will be powerless against us. If they cut off one head, two more shall take its place... [...] You are deluded, Captain... You could have the power of the gods! Yet you wear a flag on your chest and think you fight a battle of nations! I have seen the future, Captain! There are no flags!"

Johann Schmidt/Red Skull, in Captain America: The First Avenger

According to Swerdlow, the plans of the Globalists include instigating a major war starting in the Middle East, as well as staging a fake "alien invasion" to justify uniting the nations of the world under a single planetary government. Apparently, the raft of Hollywood movies with that exact scenario is designed to *program* that scenario into people's minds, so that they more readily accept it.

The Globalists' plans for the world include:

- There will be a Middle Eastern war, coupled with a world financial collapse.

- China and Israel will attack and destroy the Moslem Fundamentalists in Central and Western Asia.

- The Earth will be divided into three major political/economic units – North and South America; Europe, Africa, and the Middle East; and, the Pan-Asia/Australian region.

- A staged alien invasion will occur, forcing all nations, religions, and cultures to give up separate identities and unite under the United Nations/Global Government.

- Certain alien groups will be introduced as 'heroes' who saved the Earth.

- A New World Religion will be introduced and enforced upon all people.

- All money and assets will belong to the New Earth Empire. A Global credit system will be imposed ("cash" will be a thing of the past).

- All Earth citizens will have mandatory identification cards with their DNA imprinted upon them. These will be monitored via satellite.

- Total mind-control will be the rule of the day. Children are already being programmed into this New World Order by shows like Pokémon, Barney, Teletubbies, Ninja Turtles, and most shows on Cartoon Network and Nickelodeon.

Chapter 21: Stewart Swerdlow's Predictions (2002)

- ❏ The Dome of the Rock Mosque will be destroyed and the Temple of Solomon will be rebuilt there.

- ❏ Atlantean technology will be revealed and exploited (yes, ancient Atlantis really existed…).

- ❏ Interplanetary and interdimensional travel will openly be available to select people.

- ❏ Jupiter will become a second sun, making this a Binary Star System. This is a result of the String of Pearls Comet (technology) that struck that gas giant in 1994.

- ❏ Frozen moons of Saturn, Jupiter, and Neptune will become Earth-like after the new sun shines, and a redistribution of Earth's huge population will begin. At least three billion people will be re-colonized on at least six new "Earths."

* * * * * * * * *

These statements were published in 2002. As shocking and 'crazy' as they may appear to you at the moment (because they clash with your existing beliefs), many of the events outlined above are happening all around us!

Stewart Swerdlow explains that humanity's mind pattern of "victim mentality" is to blame for attracting tyranny. Our thoughts *attract* situations to us. But we'd rather paint ourselves as being "victims" and blame others, rather than take responsibility for our own thinking and our own decisions.

"Each person on Earth must gain control of his/her own minds to find out who and what they truly are within God-Mind. Then there will be no need

or possibility for any victim-mentality to exist, and no oppressor will be attracted. Mankind will then be free", he concludes.

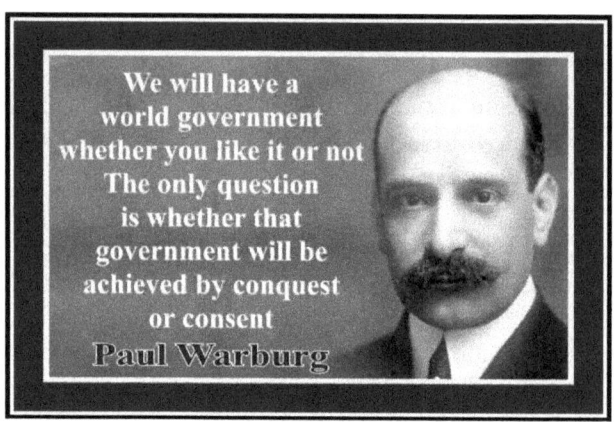

* * * * * * * * *

In December 2015, Stewart Swerdlow delivered some more predictions, during a talk he gave for his clients. He revealed:

"In the coming years… We will have the Depression caused by the global economic collapse, leading to a new global currency and a new global financial system. This will lead to a possible civil war in the USA. A former general in the US army said <u>it has been arranged for civil war to begin in South Carolina</u>. It will look like the war in Syria. There are trying to pit the people against the police.

There will be a formal announcement of the 'new Soviet Union'. The aggression of the new Soviet Union can be seen already.

There will be increased Chinese dominance in technology, politics, and entertainment. There will be mandatory vaccinations, as a result of epidemics in places like Western Africa. We will see the collapse of the EU. It will be absorbed by something else. <u>I predict</u>

Chapter 21: Stewart Swerdlow's Predictions (2002)

<u>*major food shortages and riots*</u>*, due to weather changes, war, and economic crises (I recommend you start planting and growing your own food...)."*

"We will be presented with a New World Religion after a staged 'second coming of Christ'. The Fourth Reich will emerge, out of Antarctica (the Nazis escaped there after World War II). I predict catastrophic geological events. Florida will be gone, southern Louisiana, eastern Texas...

Parts of the former continent of Lemuria will rise up in the South Pacific...

Also: Increasingly we will see robot armies and artificial intelligence computers."

* * * * * * * * *

Will Prince William Head The New World Order?

"Diana was chosen for her Merovingian bloodline secretly known as the bloodline of Christ. Throughout the ages, the Knights Templar protected the Holy bloodline until it reached its final recipient – Prince William. Even before his birth, Diana knew her fist born son was destined to be King, Messiah and leader of the New World Order."

Grace Powers, producer of the *Ring of Power* documentary

CHAPTER 22

Future Timeline Seen by Al Bielek – The Year 2137 On Earth

Alfred (Al) Bielek claims that he was part of the American military's time travel experiments in the 1940s and 1950s. These experiments were popularized in the movie *"The Philadelphia Experiment"*.

As bizarre as this sounds, numerous military insiders have backed up this story, admitting that time travel is possible and that the Secret Government have significantly more advanced technology than the general population is aware of.

They go on to explain that time is an illusion of physical reality (in the spirit world there is just a singular eternal moment of 'now'), and that all points in the Universe are connected to each other.

According to these military 'insiders', if you know the vibrational frequency of a point in the time-space continuum, you simply need to resonate an object to that frequency, for it to be transported there. This may stretch your worldview and clash with your current belief systems, but they go on to state that an advanced civilization gave this technology to the US government in exchange for certain concessions.

An interesting insight: you cannot alter history in one timeline, simply by going back in time; you would only create an alternate timeline in our multiverse (they are infinite universes and infinite possible timelines).

Bielek states that a failed experiment resulted in him travelling to the year 2137. He claims that he awoke in a hospital in the year 2137, and remained there for a few months, before being 'returned' back to our era. He described what he found out about human society in the future, as well as some of the events leading up to that era, as follows:

- There are approximately 300 million inhabitants left on the planet in 2137.

- The New World Order had failed.

- Governments are smaller and more streamlined.

- Banks' powers have been severely curtailed.

- There are changes in coastlines; for example, Florida is underwater.

- Television was showing mainly educational programs (no longer merely 'entertainment' or 'propaganda').

- Medical treatments were much more advanced. *"In hospitals they don't use '20th century medicine' anymore, but mostly holistic therapies instead, using 'vibrational' treatment and treatments using 'light'. They use much more refined surgery techniques than today"*, he stated.

Chapter 22: Future Timeline Seen by Al Bielek – The Year 2137 On Earth

- Artificial intelligence is used to aid in running governments.

- The US is under a residual of Martial Law. The civilian government is completely gone.

- There was a global war at some point between 2000 and 2100.

- Many cities didn't exist anymore (possibly due to nuclear attacks).

- The UN agenda fell by the wayside. There was no longer an attempt to create a one-world government.

- The problems started in 2003-2005. The New World Order was consolidating rapidly. But the war started between Russia and China on one side, and USA and Europe on the other. This led to nuclear attacks that wiped out a number of cities.

* * * * * * * * *

Is this really in our planet's timeline? Is this an 'alternate' timeline? The ramblings of a crazy person? Or is this merely 'propaganda' designed to make us believe that the Globalists' plans are doomed to failure and we therefore should just 'go with the flow'?

If the events outlined above actually *do* unfold over the next 100 years or so, it would definitely explain why so many 'intuitives' and psychics on our planet are seeing visions of World War III, riots and anarchy, famine, Martial Law, a vastly lowered population, and massive floods and tsunamis.

Is this the best-case scenario? That humanity will go through some horrid times but that ultimately a new consciousness will arise on our planet?

EPILOGUE

Embrace Your Spirituality, and Become Resourceful

There is no question in my mind that some major changes are about to occur on our planet. The years leading up to 2028 in particular seem fraught with turbulence.

My advice: Become a spiritual warrior. Go on a spiritual quest. Be on a spiritual journey of discovery. Be kind and loving. Become resourceful and creative. See these changing times as an incredible opportunity for growth, and an opportunity to display leadership and courage. A time for abundance and wealth, even. The coming times of war and chaos are perhaps the necessary trials Humanity needs to finally turn towards a more loving and spiritual way of life.

The Future Is Never Linear – Embrace Change

Most people think in an immature way. They are like children. They want everything to 'always be good'. They fail to realize that our Universe is one of **duality**. There can't be good without bad, light without darkness, pleasure without pain, growth without challenge, love without fear. And yet they seek to *only* experience and appreciate the love, joy, good, and pleasure of life, while rejecting all else. It is simply not a realistic way of thinking. You would be rejecting half of all Creation. Half of 'Life' itself. Embrace both sides of life. Embrace the changing cycles and the seasons of life. Embrace change. And learn from both the highs and the lows.

People have a "Normalcy Bias" – if things have been going on a certain way for long enough, they believe it will *continue* to be that way. Harry Dent writes:

> "We work hard to improve our lives and once we've reached a good place, we don't want it to end. We want to stay in that place forever. If we do move, it's only towards something bigger and better. We prefer the world to grow incrementally and in a straight line… without cycles. We reject the reality that is historically clear: that growth is both cyclical and exponential. […] We project the future in a linear way when the reality is instead both exponential and cyclical. That's why so few people can see ahead of the curve. …Unfortunately, <u>people generally don't like the play of opposites of life. We don't like the bursts that inevitably follow booms</u>, so we just pretend that life doesn't work that way. Ultimately, human beings are all about finding Nirvana and then digging in their claws to stay, no matter the consequences. […] I get it. Bubbles will always exist because life is hard, despite its rewards. Life is cyclical and challenging. It's natural to want to follow the path of least resistance, but it's not realistic. "People are unrealistic, and therefore irresponsible." […] When things are at their worst, people naturally believe that they'll never get better again. But [things do get better]."

There Is Nothing to Fear. You Are Loved Eternally

Ultimately, we never really die. Death is but an illusion, a homecoming, a rebirth. *It is physical reality that is the illusion* – a virtual reality where the soul gets to experience *life* in order to grow and evolve. There is never really anything to be afraid of.

> "Ask your oversoul and God-mind to clear the energy, to give you the guidance and knowledge for the proper actions and reactions, support in all forms, and to become a radiating beacon of unconditional love, eternal happiness, joy, peace, health, and abundance, for yourself, your loved ones, and all who seek truth. Say this to yourself 3-4 times a day, and remember: There's nothing to fear, you can't do anything wrong, you can't mess things up, you are loved eternally... you will be able to surpass everything that is going to happen to this Earth. It will be neutral, easy for you. And when you have your tests, you will need to pass them. that's when you're going to find out where you're actually at along the process. Embrace the opportunities that come your way, to see where you are at in the process." – *Stewart Swerdlow*

The Future Is Not Set in Stone. The Balance Is in Your Hands

I will leave you with these words from my friend Jamie Passmore.

> "I was told that these visions are being shown to us as a warning – <u>it doesn't mean it's necessarily going to happen</u>. The balance is in our hands... Don't focus on war, destruction... focus on creating heaven in your own life... create an amazing life for you and your family... it's about how you live on a day to day life... don't live in anger, hate... your vibrations on an individual level are

affecting the entire planet and the entire galaxy. It's a warning on what we are doing on an individual level, to help bring about a higher vibration on our planet." – *Jamie Passmore*

And remember: Live life with love in your heart. There will be a period of turbulence and change, but things *will* get better again. View these times as an opportunity to grow and to learn to love more.

> *"There's nothing to fear, you can't do anything wrong, you can't mess things up, and you are loved eternally."*

I look forward to receiving your feedback, questions, or any interesting visions and prophecies you may have had –or that you may have come across– at info@prosperitypower.com.

Epilogue: Embrace Your Spirituality, and Become Resourceful

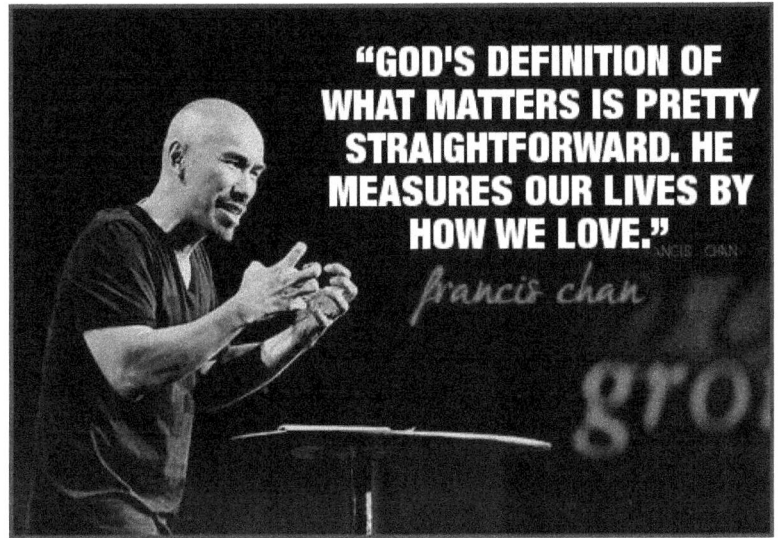

APPENDIX

A Warning About the Coming World War from Russian President Vladimir Putin

During a session with journalists at the St Petersburg International Economic Forum in June 2016, Russian President Vladimir Putin issued a stark warning about the impending threat of nuclear war.

Signed in 1972, the Anti-Ballistic Missile (ABM) Treaty barred both the US and the USSR from deploying national defenses against long-range ballistic missiles. The treaty was based on the premise that if either superpower constructed a strategic defense, the other would build up its *offensive* nuclear forces to offset the defense.

In 2002, the United States withdrew *unilaterally and without consultation* from the Treaty. President George W. Bush described the ABM Treaty as "a Cold War relic", upsetting the balance of power that – according to Putin – maintained peace in our world for 70 years. As a result, there is no instrument today in international law that prevents the possibility of mutually assured destruction.

During a Q&A session with journalists, Putin laid out in no uncertain terms the path the world's superpowers are on:

> "I must remind you that major global conflicts have been avoided in the past few decades, due to **the geostrategic balance of power, which used to exist**. The two super-nuclear powers essentially agreed to stop producing both offensive weaponry as well as defensive weaponry. It's simple how it works – where one side becomes dominant in their military potential, they are more likely to want to be the first to be able to use such power. This is the absolute linchpin to international security. The anti-missile defense system (as previously prohibited in international law), and all of the surrounding agreements that used to exist... It's not in my nature to scold someone – but when the United States unilaterally withdrew from the ABM Treaty in 1972, they delivered a colossal blow by the entire system of international security. That was the first blow, when it comes to assessing the strategic balance of power in the world.
>
> At that time (2002), I said that we will not be developing such systems also, because a) it is very expensive and b) we aren't yet sure how they will work (for the Americans.) "We're not going to burn our money." We're going to take a different option, and develop offensive weaponry, in order to retain said geo-strategic balance. That was all. Not to threaten someone else. They said – "Fine, our defense system is not against you, and we assume that your weaponry is not against us." "Do what you like!"
>
> As I already mentioned, this conversation took place in the early 2000s. Russia was in a very difficult state at that time: economic collapse... civil war and the fight against terrorism in our Caucasus region... complete destruction

of our military-industrial complex. They wouldn't have been able to imagine that Russia could ever again be a military power. My guess is they assumed that even that which was left over from the Soviet Union would eventually deteriorate. So they said, "Sure, do what you like." But we told them about the reactionary measures we were going to take. And that is what we did. And I assure you, that today, we have had every success in that area. I'm not going to list everything; all that matters is that we have modernized our military-industrial complex. And we continue to develop new generation warfare. I'm not even going to mention systems against the missile-defense system!

No matter what we said to our American partners (to curb the production of weaponry) they refused to cooperate with us, they rejected our offers and continue to do their own thing. Some things I cannot tell you right now publicly, I think that would be rude of me. And whether you believe me or not, we offered real solutions to stop this (arms race.) They rejected everything we had to offer. So here we are today - and they've placed their missile defense system in Romania. Always saying "we must protect ourselves from the Iranian nuclear threat!" Where's the threat? Where's the nuclear threat? You even have an agreement with them – and the US was the instigator of this agreement, where we helped. We supported it. But if not for the US then this agreement would not exist – which I consider Obama's achievement. I agree with the agreement, because it eased tensions in the area. So President Obama can put this in his list of achievements. So the Iranian threat does not exist. But missile defense systems are continuing to be positioned. That means we were right when we said that they are lying to us. Their reasons were not genuine, in reference to the "Iranian nuclear threat." Once again, they lied to us.

So they built this system and now they are being loaded with missiles. You, as journalists, should know that these missiles are put into capsules which are utilized from sea-based, mid-range Tomahawk rocket launchers. These are being loaded with "anti-missiles" that can penetrate distances of up to 500km. But we know that technologies advance. We even know in which year the Americans will accomplish a new missile, which will be able to penetrate distances of up to 1000km and then even further. And from that moment on they will be able to directly threaten Russia's nuclear potential.

We know year by year what's going to happen – and they know that we know. It's only you that they tell tall-tales to, and you spread it to the citizens of your other countries. **Your people, in turn, do not feel a sense of the impending danger – this is what worries me**. How can you not understand that the world is being pulled in an irreversible direction? That's the problem.

Meanwhile they pretend that nothing's going on. I don't know how to get through to you anymore. And they justify this as a "defense" system, and not weaponry that is used for the purposes of offense. Systems that "prevent aggression." This is absolutely not true. A missile defense system is one element of the whole system of offensive military potential. It works as part of a whole that includes offensive missile launchers. One complex blocks, the other launches a high precision weapon, the third blocks a potential nuclear strike and the fourth sends out its own nuclear weapon in response. This is all designed to be part of one system. This is how it works in current, non-nuclear but high precision missile defense systems.

Well okay, let's put aside the actual missile 'defense issue.' But those capsules into which 'anti-missiles' are inserted, as I've mentioned, they are sea-based. On warships which can carry the Tomahawk subsonic cruise missile system. One could deploy it to position in a matter of hours and then what kind of "anti-missile" system is that? How do we know what kind of missile is in there? All you have to do is change the program! (non-nuclear to nuclear). That's all it would take. This would happen very quickly, and even the Romanian government itself won't know what's going on. Do you think they let the Romanians call any shots? Nobody is going to know what is being done – not the Romanians, and the Polish won't either. Do you think I'm not familiar with their strategies? Ha! From what I can see, we are in grave danger. We had conversations once with our American partners – where they said they'd like to develop ballistic missiles, but without a nuclear warhead. And we said, "Do you actually understand what that might entail?" So you're going to have missiles launching from submarines, or ground territories – this is a ballistic missile – how do we know whether or not it has a nuclear warhead?! Can you even imagine what kind of scenario you can create?

But as far as I am aware, they did not go through with developing these weapons – they have paused for now. But the other one they continue to implement. I don't know how this is all going to end. What I do know is that **we will need to defend ourselves**. And I even know how they will package this "Russian aggression" again but this is simply our response to your actions. Is it not obvious that I must guarantee the safety of our people?

And not only that, but we must attempt to regain the necessary strategic balance of power, which is that point that I began with. Let me return to it, in order to finish my response. It was precisely this balance of power that guaranteed the safety of humanity from major global conflict, over the past 70 years. It was a blessing rooted in a "mutual threat" but this mutual threat is what guaranteed mutual peace, on a global scale. How they could so easily tear it down, I simply don't know. I think this is gravely dangerous. I not only think that, I am assured of it."

Napoleon and Hitler tried to invade Russia from Europe. The US and NATO are massing troops and supposed "anti-missile" systems close to the Russian border currently. Iran is incensed by the presence of American frigates in the Persian Gulf. China is fuming about the presence of America's Seventh Fleet in the South China Sea... It is understandable that the Russian leadership feels their nation is being encircled, threatened and provoked, and feels that it must develop weapons to protect its citizens.

Or is this just propaganda designed to justify future aggression from Russia and China?

Whatever the case may be, it is the *people* who will suffer the consequences of the coming war – on both sides of the conflict.

Harry S. Dent's Predictions: Real Estate Will Crash 60%, The Stock Market Will Crash 80 to 90%

Although Harry S. Dent is not 'psychic', his predictions have been so accurate over the past 25 years that he might as well be. He is a highly successful economic prognosticator, and the author of the bestselling books *The Roaring 2000s, The Great Depression Ahead, and The Demographic Cliff*. He is one of only a handful of people who accurately predicted the stock market boom of the early 2000s, as well as the 2008 crash, in contrast to almost every economist, 'talking head', and financial 'expert' out there.

In his recent book *The Sale of a Lifetime*, Harry Dent made the following predictions:

Real estate prices will crash 50 to 60% in the US and Europe, 30 to 40% in Australia and as much as 80% in China... *"January 2000 is the benchmark for real estate prices. We're about to see another six-year slide that will take home prices back, at least, to their early 2000 levels, where the bubble began. If you have the courage, look up the value of your home or real estate in January 2000! You will be shocked at your downside potential... [...] Since this bubble, starting in early 2000, is so extreme, it won't just burst back to normal levels (adjusted for inflation). It's likely to go even lower! After that, it will resume its natural trend of little or no appreciation outside of inflation. In short, real estate will never be the same again. It can't be. Not with slowing demographic trends. More people are dying and thus selling than younger people are buying in more and more wealthy, developed countries.*

Regarding **the US stock market**, he states: *"Things could go down to 1994 prices – late 1994 [when the bubble started]. That's where I see* things going to, or maybe lower." "The US stock market will be down 30%... We are going to see another meltdown in most stock markets, by mid-October. Be out of stocks, out of real estate. Be cash-rich. [...] ...I believe we're looking at a **Dow 3,800 or a bit lower by 2020-2022** — to go back to where it started in early 1995 — once this bubble has fully unwound. Most of that crash is likely to come by late 2017... I expect the Dow to fall to around 5,500 by late 2017."

"The Great Depression of 2016-2022 – mark my words here: later 2016 and 2017 will see the worst stock decline since 1930-1932 (and 1973-1974) and this next Great Depression will last into the end of the demographically based down season, around late 2022. We'll see the worst coming into early 2020, when all four of my key macroeconomic cycles are still pointing down together. It will be brutal, especially after such unprecedented monetary policies... [...] before the trends turn back up between early 2020 and late 2022."

It is worth mentioning that Robert Kiyosaki, in his 2002 book *Rich Dad's Prophecy: Why the Biggest Stock Market Crash in History Is Still Coming*... predicted that a major stock market crash would occur in 2016…

Harry Dent anticipates that **at least 100 TRILLION dollars in financial assets could disappear** in the next few years. *"You'll have deflation... because there will be less money and assets chasing after the available goods and services…"* "Prices of goods from China will go down (massive deflation). They have massive excess capacity. Wait for prices to go down, and stock up. Everything is going down (prices). Make sure you have things that are strategic to you (stock up), in case there is some dislocation in global trade." "I like to compare bubbles to magic. They create money and wealth out of thin air. And then all that artificial money and wealth disappears in the blink of an eye. "Now you see it, now you don't!" …When loans go bad, all the money created disappears, including your deposits. It happened in the great deflation of the early 1930s. It will happen again in this next great deflation from 2017 to 2023."

He is expecting the bubbles in asset prices – created by massive money-printing by central banks, euphemistically called 'Quantitative Easing' – to burst: *"I've never seen bubbles like this. And this China bubble is off the charts… the commodities bubble burst… the China bubble… the US subprime bubble earlier..."* He adds: *"People are dumb. They love bubbles. Speculating. People love getting something for nothing... […] The reality is we're greedy bastards who want to get rich quick, with no effort. So when everyone starts doing something, it looks less risky…"*

Dent expects unrest in the US, China, and Europe: *"Australia and New Zealand would be my #1 place to live, during this crisis. There's less polarity in your culture (social division) than in the US. Much higher civil unrest potential in USA and China. Prepare for the worst. Store some water. Unemployment, crime, and civil unrest go hand in hand." "[The Australian] government is less in debt and better able to deal with the coming crisis. And you have a very civil society that will see less unrest than China or the U.S. I have said this many times before, and will repeat it here again: if I had to choose one developed country to sit out this crisis, it would be Australia (with New Zealand a close runner up)."*

Currencies: *"The Australian currency will go to $0.60 to the dollar"* (note: it was at parity 1:1 a couple of years ago, currently at $0.75…). *"The euro should be at parity [with the dollar]."* Oil prices: *"I think oil could be down to $30-$32 a barrel."*

The price of Gold: *"Inflation is falling around the world. Gold keeps going down. It usually bounces in the early stages of a crisis. <u>I am predicting that Gold will be $700-740 by late 2016, early 2017</u>… going all the way down to $250. Gold goes up in an <u>inflation</u> crisis. Gold is not the place to protect yourself now. Gold is not a currency. […] Ultimately, gold is likely to bottom around $400 between 2020 and 2022 when the clockwork-like, 30-Year Commodity Cycle turns back up again. At its worst, it could go back to its 2001 low of $250 before seeing a long-term boom again, led by emerging countries. Gold could hit $3,000, even $5,000, in the next 30-*

Year Commodity Cycle peak... but that will only be around 2038-2040... [...] Gold started going exponential in 2005, from $400 upward. So again, $400 is the most likely bottom target." It will be interesting to see if this particular prediction will come to pass. Many experts predict that the price of Gold and Silver will reach $10,000 and $240 an ounce, respectively (up from $1,300 and $19 currently)... so who is right? Time will tell.

Dent expects things to get better after 2023: *"...The recovery that we'll see around 2020 – 2023 forward, after the greatest depression and deflationary bubble burst in history... The next several years are a once-in-a-lifetime opportunity to create extreme wealth in your investments and business if you act against the grain... [...] Despite the crisis, this presents the once-in-a-lifetime opportunity to create extreme wealth in a short period of time... if you see it coming. A small proportion of people are going to make a FORTUNE when this bubble bursts. Most people are going to be walking around in a daze, like, 'What happened?' My house went down 60%. I'm underwater on my mortgage. I can't refinance. 'I lost my job. All my neighbours lost their jobs. My kids can't get a job..."*

Harry Dent's advice during a recent webinar: *"<u>Sell stocks, hold the money in cash or safe bonds.</u> I bought Treasury bonds. The dollar is a safe haven currency. When things go down you'll be able to buy anything of real value at unbelievably low prices. You can also short stocks. You can have options, they're very cheap right now, to hedge your stocks and real estate investments. Major bubbles occur only about once in a human lifetime, so it is easy to forget the lessons from the last one. If you're looking to buy your first house, wait until 2017 or even a few years later. If looking to sell your business, do so ASAP. Wait for the major crash to start re-investing, longer term 2020 – 2022 is best. Not before then. Business Strategies: cash and cash flow are critical to surviving the shake-out and having the resources to take advantage of unprecedented bargains in financial assets in the years ahead (2015-2020). Be lean and mean. Focus on cutting fixed costs and overheads. Identify weak competitors and their assets that you will be able to buy for 20 cents on the dollar... Then: Buy India, Mexico, Southeast Asia, Health Care, Starter Homes and Vacation Homes."*

The Great Global Monetary Reset

Brandon Smith of Alt-Market.com is one of the few truly insightful news commentators out there. He recently made the following predictions, in an article titled *What Will The Global Economy Look Like After The "Great Reset"?*

❑ *"The globalists ultimately want to diminish or* **erase the U.S. dollar as the world reserve currency.**"

❑ *"They want to consolidate economic governance, moving away from a franchise system of national central banks into* **a single global monetary authority**, *most likely under the IMF or the Bank for International Settlements."*

❑ *"They consistently argue for* **the centralization of political power.**"

❑ *"One or more of these catalysts will be triggered: a Saudi de-peg from the U.S. dollar, a large scale terrorist attack, a general rout in stock markets due to a loss of faith in central bank policy, a confrontation between Eastern and Western powers. It doesn't really matter much. All of it is* **designed to produce one outcome — chaos.** *To which the globalists will offer 'order', their particular order using their particular solutions as 'objective mediators'."*

❑ *"In our highly interdependent system in the West in which more than 80 percent of the population has been domesticated and is psychologically incapable of self-reliance, it is very likely that* **a disruption of normal supply chains and services would result in considerable poverty and death.** *Such* a threat would invariably lead frightened and unprepared people to demand increased government controls..."

- "One important factor to note is the rationale globalists will offer for increased centralization and control in the hands of a few... [...] In Casti's theory (more propaganda than theory), collapse is inevitable in what he calls "overly complex systems." The more independent elements within any system, the more chance there is for unpredictable events that lead to supposed disaster. Ostensibly, the solution would be to streamline all systems and remove the free-radicals. That is to say, complete centralization is the answer. What a surprise. **Centralization will be championed as the cure-all** to the barbaric relic of complexity."

- "You are going to see long standing financial institutions sacrificed in the name of rehabilitating the global system. Do not assume that certain major banks (Deutsche Bank?) will not be brought down, or that certain central banks will not be toppled (Federal Reserve) as the reset progresses. Also do not assume even that certain geopolitical structures will not be brought into disarray (European Union)."

- "...the legalized confiscation of bank accounts, pension funds, stock holdings, etc. as a method for prolonging a collapse event. [...] Some people (socialists/communists) may even cheer the action as the end of 'capitalism'."

- "It is important to realize that currency devaluation will probably occur across the board in every region of the world. Some currencies will simply be hit harder than others. The dollar is a primary target of the globalists and WILL be brought down."

- "Many necessities and the means to produce those necessities will skyrocket in cost. There may not be inflation in every sector of the economy because imploding demand could offset some of the effects *of falling currency value, but there will be* **extreme inflation in the areas that hurt common people most.**"

❑ *"Consolidation Of Government Power: …It is highly unlikely that the global reset will result in a collapse of government. On the contrary, it is usually during economic collapse that* **governments grow in power to the point of totalitarianism.***"*

❑ *"Production of goods on the massive scale seen today will not ever be allowed to return if the elites have their way. This will create a perpetual lack of supply (by design). The only methods for dealing with lost production on an industrial level would be to either encourage localized production in every community, or to force people to reduce their standard of living and demand in the extreme. The elites will certainly press for the latter."*

❑ *"… I believe they will attempt to make any local production impossible, first through taxation … and second, by confiscation of raw resources needed to manufacture goods on a scale that would grow wealth for a community. The government will claim that such resources must be managed by the authorities for the good of everyone rather than 'wasted' by independent businesses in the 'pursuit of personal wealth'. Eventually, they will also have to limit or outlaw barter and alternative currencies in order for the digitized economy to work."*

❑ *"In order to fully centralize, the elites must streamline. […] This means greatly diminished production, but also by extension* **greatly diminishing the population.** *Population controls then become vital."*

Read the full article at www.alt-market.com

Prophecy 2017 – 2137

Psychic Hollywood: Is Hollywood Warning Us of What Is To Come?

Is Hollywood using psychics' predictions of the future to come up with movie ideas? Or are Hollywood's dystopian images programming our minds and manifesting an apocalyptic outcome into our reality?

Hollywood spent billions of dollars since the 1980s to produce movies featuring terrorism. Examples include: *Die Hard, The Siege, Body of Lies, The Kingdom, The Dark Knight, True Lies, Air Force One, Unthinkable, The Sum of All Fears, Spy Game, Olympus Has Fallen, World Trade Center, The Devil's Own, From Paris with Love, Swordfish, Patriot Games, In the Name of the Father, Executive Decision, Under Siege, The Delta Force, The Peacemaker, Flight 93, Rendition, The Dark Knight Rises, Homeland Security, Zero Dark Thirty, Lions for Lambs, Day of the Jackal, Argo, Syriana, Back To The Future, Broken Arrow, The Rock, Skyfall, Speed, The World Is Not Enough, Captain America, The Avengers, Iron Man, Suicide Squad…* the list goes on.

For some reason, it seems we are also being conditioned for **the scenario of an 'alien invasion'**: *The 5th Wave, 10 Cloverfield Lane, Alien Raiders, Arrival, The Avengers, Battle: Los Angeles, Battleship, The Fourth Kind, Oblivion, Pacific Rim, Pixels, Signs, Skyline, Star Wars, Man of Steel, Independence Day, Mars Attacks, Invasion of the Body Snatchers, Teenage Mutant Ninja Turtles, Dark Skies, The Day The Earth Stopped, Cowboys & Aliens, War of the Worlds, Edge of Tomorrow, Avatar, Ender's Game, Star Trek, Men in Black, The World's End, Predator, Home, The Host, The X-Files, Monsters, V, Evolution, Childhood's End, Transformers, Transformers: The Revenge of the Fallen, Transformers: Age of Extinction…*

What is particularly worrying is that <u>practically every movie about the future of America presents a vision that is dystopian and apocalyptic</u>, with scenes of nuclear fallout, famine, violence, crime, civil war, Martial Law, mass casualties and mass depopulation. Some more examples include: *The Hunger Games, I Am Legend, The Purge, The Purge: Anarchy, The Purge: Election Year, The Road, The Matrix, Terminator, Divergent, The Book of Eli, Children of Men, Mad Max: Fury Road, Tomorrowland, Captain America: Civil War, Batman vs Superman, World War Z, 2012, This is The End, Robocop, Snowpiercer, The High-Rise…*

Is Hollywood preparing the American public and the world for an extremely bleak future? Why are they planting that apocalyptic vision of the world in the minds of every human being on Earth? Humans are so 'programmed' for an apocalyptic dystopian future that they are manifesting it with their thoughts. Why aren't we ever presented with <u>a vision of a better world in the future, one with more abundance and personal freedom</u>?

In the movie *X-Men: Apocalypse*, the tagline of the movie is **"Only The Strong Will Survive".** Are they warning us of what is about to come? The movie name-checks The Four Horsemen of the Apocalypse, and the villain is called *En Sabah Nur* (which is Turkish for "The Morning Light" or "Lucifer"). After being awakened from his underground tomb by his followers, thousands of years after he was betrayed and thrown into this pit, he declares that he will *"purge the world… lay waste to the world in a day of reckoning…"* to then build a better world.

These are direct quotes from the movie's villain, 'Apocalypse' or *En Sabah Nur*:

- *"The weak have taken the Earth. For this, I was betrayed. False gods. Idols. No more. I have returned. The new tomorrow, that starts today..."*
- *"This world needs to be... Purged."*
- *"I was there to spark and fan the flame of man's awakening, to spin the wheel of civilization. And when the forest would grow rank and in need of clearing for new growth... I was there to set it ablaze."*
- *"I was Asleep. Trapped in darkness. I was not there for you, my son. But I am here now."*
- *"Everything they've built will fall! And from the ashes of their world, we'll build a better one!"*
- *"Tell them that this Earth will be laid waste. That it is I, En Sabah Nur, who wreak this upon them."*
- *"You have lost your way. But I have returned. The day of reckoning, it is here… All your buildings and temples... will fall. The dawn of a new era will emerge."*
- *"You will reach deep into the Earth. Rip everything they built from the ground. Wipe clean this world. And we will lead those that survived… into to a better one."*

This movie might appear to the casual observer to be mere spectacle, with a nonsensical storyline, but it is eerily similar to the story of how Lucifer (humanity's true God, according to certain secret society insiders) was betrayed and cast into the Inner Earth.

Other quotes in the movie include:

- ❑ *"En Sabah Nur... named after an ancient being they believed to be the world's first... mutant. They believe that the first mutant was born ten of thousands of years ago. And they believe he will rise again."* [they expect Lucifer to rise again?]
- ❑ *"I saw the end of the world. I could feel all this death..."*
- ❑ *"... to break forth bloodily, then the past must be obliterated and a new start made. Let us now start fresh, without remembrance..."*
- ❑ *"What we're seeing is a magnetic phenomenon on a much larger scale than we saw in Auschwitz..."* [more death than in Auschwitz?]
- ❑ *"Eventually, cities, urban centers. Anything built since the Bronze Age will be wiped away. The death toll will be billions."*
- ❑ *"... If he does that, he'll have the power to control every mind in the world..."*
- ❑ *"They took everything away from me. Now... We'll take everything from them."*
- ❑ *"The Pentagon has confirmed <u>multiple launches from Russia, as well as the UK, Israel and China. So far, there has been no response from the White House</u>..."*

The theme of 'Lucifer arising' is presented allegorically in many popular movies in recent years, including: Lucy [*Lucifer*], Jupiter Ascending (*a.k.a. Lucifer Ascending*), The Dark Knight Rises (*Dark Knight = 'Lord of Darkness'*), Lucifer (TV series), Transformers: The Revenge of The Fallen (*where the evil Megatron is retrieved from the abyss and brought back to life by his followers*), Transformers: Age of Extinction (*this refers to the extinction of mankind, to purify the Earth...*), Transmorphers: The Fall of Man...

In the 2016 movie *Suicide Squad*, the character named 'Enchantress' decides to eradicate humankind with a mystical weapon, as a punishment for imprisoning her.

In the 2015 movie *The Fantastic Four*, superhuman Victor von Doom is retrieved from Planet Zero by his followers, and brought back to Earth. *Believing the human race needs to be destroyed so he can rebuild the planet in his image*, he starts killing soldiers and scientists...

In the 2015 TV series *Childhood's End*, aliens ('The Overlords') arrive on Earth on a spaceship and disarm the world's armies. While not showing themselves, over a period of a few years they share advanced technology with Mankind and help usher in a decades-long era of prosperity, health, longevity, peace, and cooperation on our planet. Eventually their leader reveals himself to be... the Devil  (Lucifer). The children around the world smile when they see him appear on TV for the first time. When questioned about why he looks like the Devil from the Bible, he explains that the Bible was wrong: *"After all, not all religions can be right."* Shortly thereafter, all the human children are taken off-world and planet Earth is annihilated by The Overlords.

In the 2013 movie *Man of Steel*, the superhuman general Zod vows to exterminate humanity, turn Earth into a new Krypton, and build a society of genetic purity.

In the X-Men movies, the character 'Magneto' makes references about a future war between the X-Men and the humans, where the humans are destined to lose and be wiped out because they are 'inferior'.

See the common theme, there? At the very least, Hollywood scriptwriters are taking inspiration from the Bible's "End of Days" prophecies.

In the 2014 movie *The Purge*, "The New Founding Fathers of America" have been voted into office following economic collapse… The two sequels in 2015 and 2016 are titled *'Anarchy'* and *'Election Year'*…

"HYDRA was founded on the belief that humanity could not be trusted with its own freedom… Humanity needed to surrender its freedom willingly… For seventy years HYDRA has been secretly feeding crisis, reaping war. And when history did not cooperate, history was changed… HYDRA created a world so chaotic that humanity is finally ready to sacrifice its freedom to gain its security. Once the purification process is complete, HYDRA's New World Order will arise. We won, Captain."

Dr. Arnim Zola – Captain America: The Winter Soldier

In the 2016 movie *The 5th Wave*, a city-sized alien spaceship is circling Earth… the aliens unleash their '1st Wave', an electromagnetic pulse that permanently destroys all electrical power on Earth, including shorting out all vehicles and causing aircraft to fall from the sky…. The 2nd Wave sees them manipulate the Earth's fault lines, causing massive earthquakes and gigantic tsunamis that kill those living in the world's coastal cities… In the 3rd Wave, they weaponize a strain of avian flu, using Earth's billions of birds as carriers of the virus, killing most of what remains of the world's population… In the 4th wave, the adults are massacred by the army (the military is 'possessed' by the aliens)… The 5th wave involves using deception to trick the rescued human children into killing the surviving humans…

In the 2014 movie *Kingsman: The Secret Service*, the villain uses technology that makes everyone across the whole world want to kill each other (similar to the prophetic visions of a 'zombie virus' we've mentioned earlier…). In the movies *I Am Legend, World War Z*, and dozens more, a virus turns humans into 'zombies' and wipes out most of humanity.

The 2006 film *Children of Men* takes place in 2027, where two decades of human infertility have left society on the brink of collapse. Illegal immigrants seek sanctuary in the United Kingdom, where the last functioning government remains (implying that there is chaos and anarchy throughout the world…).

In the 2015 movie *High-Rise*, the residents at the top floors of a high-rise (the 'Elite' of society) hoard most of the building's resources and plot against the lower-floor residents. The ensuing 'civil unrest' and riots in the building kills off most of the lower-floor residents. The High-Rise building is an allegory for our human society, with the ruling class families 'at the top'.

Practically every line of dialogue in this movie hints at the need for *depopulation*:

- *"Women around here would help the planet more by keeping their legs crossed."*
- *"He [Architect Anthony Royal] is intent on colonising the skies. Can't blame him, seeing what is happening at street level…"*
- *"All the floors below the 12th were out of power…"*
- *"I conceived this building as a crucible for change,"* [Anthony Royal] confesses. *"I must've missed some vital element."*
- The janitor: *"Look. If you lower people keep overloading the system, there are going to be cuts."* Answer from an indignant lower-floor resident: *"Who are you calling 'people'?!"*
- (lower-floor resident) *"I have no qualms about invasions of my privacy by government agencies or data processing organisations. All I want is my fair share of the electricity so I can turn a damn light on around here."*
- *"We are all bio-robots now. None of us can live without the equipment we surround ourselves with."*
- *"I suspect Laing here has been charged with disseminating propaganda amongst the lower orders… dangling a carrot of friendship… and approval."*
- *"There's no food left… only the dogs…"*
- *"Some people are bartering wives for food, on lower floors…"*
- *"This whole place obviously needs… a firmer hand. […] We can't have a repeat of last night… We need to show the lower floors that we can throw a better party than them… We must prevail… First thing first: we must commandeer all necessary resources… […] We'd like you to lead a delegation… to the supermarket."*

- ❑ *"Once we dispense with the likes of Wilder, we play the lower people off against each other another… In short: Balkanize the central section, then begin colonisation of the entire building. Then, I propose Royal draw up plans to remodel the lower floors." […] "Who knows… perhaps [this high rise] will become a paradigm of future developments…"*

- ❑ *"Sit back and wait for failure to reach the second tower of this high rise development, ready to welcome its residents into this New World… with open arms."*

- ❑ *"Now that so many of the residents were out of the way, he felt able to relax…"*

- ❑ *"One thing's for sure, this building is nowhere near as modern as some would like to think… Sometimes he found it difficult not to believe they were living in a future that had already taken place."*

There are also scenes of riots in the High-Rise's supermarket, empty supermarket shelves, the water supply to the lower floors is stopped, the inhabitants eat dog food and eventually eat their pet dogs in order to survive *(this is happening in Venezuela at the moment, where a dozen eggs, if you can find any, cost $150…)*. In the movie, there is a 9pm-7am curfew, and electricity to the lift is only available 4 hours a day. A license plate is shown that reads 'WEA610M'. Does it signify 'we are 610 million'?

Finally, as I mentioned before, in the 2014 Tom Cruise movie *The Edge of Tomorrow*, the movie ends with this announcement in a news broadcast heard in the background, after the aliens are defeated: **"Russian and Chinese forces are marching across Europe without resistance."**

What does Hollywood know that they are not telling us? Or *are* they, in fact, *telling us?*

A Message From Jesus Christ, Channelled by a Prophet

The following is a transcript of a prophetic message by a man of extraordinary psychic insight, who prefers to remain anonymous. The following statements were made on September 27th 2015:

"I sit here and think of you, I think of all of your hearts and souls. I am here to give you a message.

I am here now because I am needed. I channel my words through my only messenger of the Earth for his name will be left without a face as the devil lives within many who wish to crucify his very being. But he is a man that you will know, a man that has and will continue to perform miracles of the body and visions of insight. Follow this man when he is shown to you. He is my eyes and my voice. We the divine angels and the holy existence have not forsaken you. We have never left your side.

We have been planning great outcomes in the place of man and women, outcomes that will overcome the sadness and hatred and disillusion within the people of the Earth. But you as people must stand together and do the work of my father, God himself.

Valiant I was as a man, I am now the Holy Spirit. I am the prayers and sun the stars and the love you hold within. I am the messenger from my father and the truth to all that love me. I am Christ.

I have a sadness of heart because of the sadness that man has created. Why did man not listen to what I have foretold of my past. Why has man left love and divinity to walk with greed and a selfish heart? Why is doubt within such a force from the depths of Satan himself?

Why do you talk of me but do not truly walk the path of my words? You desire me yet you do not save yourselves. You live in hope that I will arrive at the gates of your home yet you do not do my work. You wish for divine love, but yet within you walk a life where grace has become nullified, yet I am here. Here within a man of the Earth.

Over the coming months the earth will shake, the rains will fall and many lives will be lost. The skies will darken and the force of evolution will be upon all. The lands, which many walk, will be paved with blood from the force of evil that exists within the fallen men through fallen religion. Many will try to find sanctuary but man has made it so it will not be possible. In the year of 2016 many will perish at the hands of steel and fire. The men who lead the world will be behind it. The men who stand at the helm of your life will create new messages to the masses creating more sadness among many. The men of power are not driven just by greed but by the worship of the dark. What you see is not to be trusted. They have created plans which will bring chaos to the world, as you will soon know, for the greater good of only a few.

Religious leaders have planned a great shift and move to control the weary and the poor, and with this will hope to control the masses at the peril of many. As the 4th moon comes in the second month of 2016 the true Holy war has begun. The fight between good and evil is at the foot of many and only the true that walk with the divine will find sanctuary and guidance from my father within. Walls and divides will become more present over the coming months to keep people in a place of solitude. People of the Earth will become hungry and forgotten, governments will rise and become leaders of the dark.

The time is not lost, the time is yours again, but you must listen to my words. If you doubt my words I will walk away far into the sun, and far from reach. I have come as I said, not as you thought. The moments written and now in the eyes of many is now of this month, it is what is happening right now as you listen to me speak. The previous prophecies are not wrong, but seen in the wrong light. The reader must look again so see the vision in the correct way. The reader must understand that I am here now, that I am here to guide you when my father decides so.

The reader needs to understand that he, who seeks the truth into my divine heart will lead the way with a selfless mind to overcome the end of all. The reader must not convert him or herself into ways of Allah unless walking with Love of the heart. One must be apparent in the almighty as God himself. There must not be many religions to speak of. The men who walk in the name of Allah are at a crossing within. The words of the dark are filtering though the mind and within the eyes of many across the Earth to create sadness among many. Allah is a true God, a true God of his word but the people who walk with malice are not. Allah will forgive but only those who keep the word of his grace. Allah will, as when speaking to me turn his back on the force of darkness upon the Earth. This will happen in a rage of power from the force of the leaders of the world. Listen closely to the gentle ways of the east, but the eastern ways must also be one of peace or forgotten amongst the sadness to follow.

Do not believe that you are safe without the divine within. Do not believe that it is only I who needs to save the soul that you walk with.

Do not believe that the devil is not among you. Do not believe that the people of government who lead you will save you.
Do not believe that life in the conscious state is all that is to be found. Do not believe in just prayer but action of strength of heart to find peace.

Do not believe in the man who stands inside the church but asks for money. Do not believe the righteous who stand with my name but stand for reason of self-egotism.

Do not believe the pathway is clear for you to walk unless walking with the divine. Do not believe that without love you can still find solace. Do not believe in the men who talk of me as though I am they.

You must join together as people of the world to find harmony and do so before it is too late. I am here to show you light within your soul and to bring you hope of a new time that is soon to come. A beautiful sun will shine across the skies of many a heart and I will forgive the lost. I come to grant you messages from my father to show you a divine pathway that has been lost for many moons and sacred times.

You must not let the sadness of man create judgment of others. You must not let the evil that stands by your side take over your strength. You must not let the unfortunate fall victim to the tyranny of government, you must stand with your fellow men and women and support Love.

You must be the holder of the key to your own divine awareness and strive to define a place for yourself, within the time and life you are living at present. You must not follow the corrupt soul to the find earthly physical for this will end the earth as you know it.

You must not breath the words of hatred to religion for this will continue to bring more holy war and much sacrifice throughout your land. You must not fear that I am not with you as I am already here within a man of the earth.

You must look to the stars and the heavens to understand the future of the new beginning for here lays many truths to biblical statements. You must cradle the poor and build bridges to form heart, soul and awareness of the divine to achieve the desires of my Father himself.

You must walk as I did, free of greed to find the truth of wealth of your spirit.

You must not allow the evil man of the world to dictate your future, you must stand tall and with that know that I am here with you. You must find solutions to the problems that live within the place of religion and overcome the fear that it has created within you. You must strive to come together as one race of people no matter the colour or creed. Do not be discouraged as you must have faith in me, walk with me and be guided in your hearts by me. You must no longer listen to the words of previous scripture but my voice of today. This is the message you have been waiting for. The non-believer will be left aside of my path as now is the time to stand together and the space in which time is becoming smaller as I say these words to all of you.

You must follow me as I speak these words to you. You must remove your doubt and you will find me again. If you believe in me you will feel me within you and around you as you listen to me speak these words to you. You will see your life start to become more positive and happiness arrive within your heart. You will notice things start to change within your life for the better and very soon after listening to my words. But you must believe in me, know that I am Christ and that I am here once again. God bless you all."

www.ingramcontent.com/pod-product-compliance
Lightning Source LLC
Chambersburg PA
CBHW051926160426
43198CB00012B/2055